W9-BIC-192

Marketing Illustration
New Venues, New Styles, New Methods

by Steven Heller and Marshall Arisman

© 2008 Steven Heller and Marshall Arisman

All rights reserved. Copyright under Berne Copyright Convention, Universal Copyright Convention, and Pan-American Copyright Convention. No part of this book may be reproduced, stored in a retrieval system, or transmitted in any form, or by any means, electronic, mechanical, photocopying, recording, or otherwise, without prior permission of the publisher.

12 11 10 09 08   5 4 3 2 1

Published by Allworth Press
An imprint of Allworth Communications, Inc.
10 East 23rd Street, New York, NY 10010

Cover design by James Victore, Inc.
Interior design by Shawn Hasto
Page composition/typography by Integra Software Services, Pvt., Ltd., Pondicherry, India

Library of Congress Cataloging-in-Publication Data
Heller, Steven.
    Marketing illustration: new venues, new styles, new methods / by Steven Heller and Marshall Arisman.—1st ed.
        p. cm.
    Includes index.
    ISBN-13: 978-1-58115-657-7
    ISBN-10: 1-58115-657-X
    1. Commercial art.   2. Commercial art—Marketing.   I. Arisman, Marshall.
        II. Title.
    NC1001.H46 2008
    741.6068'8—dc22

                                                                    2008050224

Printed in the United States of America

Table of Contents

Acknowledgements

We are indebted to Tad Crawford, publisher, for his continued support of illustration and our books on the subject. Thanks also to Bob Porter, associate publisher, for his enthusiasm, and to Janet Robbins, our editor on this project.

Nothing could be accomplished without the persistent aid of Kim Ablondi, whose managerial skills are invaluable to our projects.

Gratitude goes to David Rhodes, President of the School of Visual Arts, for allowing the School of Visual Arts to co-publish this and our other volumes. And to Anthony Rhodes for his continued support.

Thanks also to all those who cooperated and responded to our many requests for information and insight. This book is dedicated to those illustrators and educators who passionately work in this historic field.

—SH & MA

Foreword

To market, to market, to buy a fat pig,
Home again, home again, dancing a jig;
To market, to market, to buy a fat hog;
Home again, home again, jiggety-jog;
To market, to market, to buy a plum bun,
Home again, home again, market is done.

If only it was this easy to market your illustration. But given the changes in the field over the past decade, the traditional outlets have become more difficult to break into and the newer ones are a bit more enigmatic than they should be.

This is no Mother Goose book, but rather a guide for the young or old illustrator who wonders what the best routes are for selling work, getting assignments, and reaching an audience. You will see that conventional and unconventional methods are both current. The market has been opened to a wide range of genres and methods, so once you've finished this book, we urge you to jiggety-jog your way to whichever market is the most open for your specific talents.

Introduction

What an Illustrator Wants: A Letter to the Editors

It may seem odd to begin a book on marketing and the future of illustration with a letter from a student, but having received scores of these annually, we've come to believe they are indicative of both the insecurities and the hopes of those thousands who enter the field every year. This particular letter is not unusual, but it is extremely articulate. It reads almost like a manifesto, so when it arrived, we felt it would be the perfect introduction to this book.

Dear Sir,

My name is Brian Markle. I am from Seattle and I attend Cornish College of the Arts. I am a student illustrator right now; I begin my senior year this fall, and I have reached an obstruction in my field and am feeling a little disconcerted. I am a well-educated designer, and I think in terms of design, but I answer my problems with illustration.

Yet why is it that illustrators very rarely get the lucrative conceptual work designers get? Exhibition design, information design, environmental design, social design, campaign design, academic design; I have practiced and studied all of these components of design, but on every project, I end up with illustration and clean type.

The drawings differ. I do not have a consistent style, and I work in motion and Web as well. I laugh at this semi-existential crisis within my field, but it does concern me, because I know that the success of an illustrator weighs heavily on his or her notoriety for a certain style.

So I ask, Can illustrators be known for a more conceptual and process-based practice, or should they rely on maintaining a certain aesthetic?

This sounds like a rather trite problem for a student, because I do know that illustration and design can be quite often one and the same. But what about those illustrators who want to be considered *illustrators*? This is my problem, which relates to my intended thesis this spring.

I want my thesis to deal with the "new" illustrator. The illustrators of today should no longer have to be subject to trends that cause their jobs to become rather short-lived. Instead, I would like to see illustrators become more known not only for their process, but also their content value. When I say content value I am referring to what we choose to draw, not how we draw.

Great illustrators, to me, are supreme designers, for they cherish clarity of image but they also handle that clarity in an infinite number of illustrative ways for various clients and formats. Their work goes beyond good drawing; it is just damn good thinking.

Yet for some of these illustrators, their work lives in the world of typical illustration (i.e., music, books, editorials, and advertising). Rarely do you see a great illustrator on the front of a huge social campaign, a conceptual exhibit, academic/research work, environmental design, or info-graphics.

And I know the theories for this. I cherish type as much as I do illustration and I respect simplicity and reductive logic within my drawings, but I feel like what is truly missing in the theories of modernism and functional design is FUN! Fun can be the single component to make everything work. And it can be a highly employable trait, much like a good illustrator who is known for watercolors. Paul Rand knew this, which is why people acknowledged him for his thinking, but overlooked his simple, brilliant drawing style.

So I ask again, Can illustrators be known for a more conceptual and process-based practice, or should they rely on maintaining a certain aesthetic?

If you read this, thank you so much for your time. Any advice or words you can contribute would be greatly appreciated.

—Brian Markle

Preface

What an Illustrator Will Get:
A Letter From the Editors

What Brian Markle wants (as do most illustrators) is respect. That is not in our power as authors to provide, but we can offer suggestions and alternatives on how to get work. Illustration has long been a second cousin to design, although it was once—in the early twentieth century—its uncle. Given the current surge in the marketplace for visual entertainment, from graphic novels to video games to animated films to toys and streetwear, the role of the illustrator is decidedly more significant as a generator of content and of profit. With this comes new definitions for illustration and illustrator. This book reports on that shift in emphasis, as well as on the maintenance of the status quo.

We are addressing the nuts and bolts of marketing your work and yourself. Through the authors and others, the blueprint of how to launch a career will be provided and systematically explained.

This book is not going to be a panacea for malaise, nor will it wipe away any frustrations over the so-called demise of illustration, but learning what we've learned might boost the spirits of those who have heard such rumors. To understand where the field is, we have assembled a number of illustrators to discuss their work and where the field is headed. In answers to our survey, they discuss what they are doing now and how much of their work is "untraditional" or "traditional," and you'll be surprised by the responses. In "Teaching Illustration Today" (page 191), five major illustration department chairs talk about what they look for in a student, and what the student, in turn, looks for in a program. We address how to market the new illustration and where those markets are, and we talk to a few veteran illustrators about the field they entered and how it has changed since.

What should you take away from this book? The belief that you have a future in illustration, and the belief that *illustration* has a future.

Chapter One

What to Do If You *Want* to Make Art, But *Need* to Make A Living

Throughout the twentieth century, the obvious solution to this particular quandary was to compromise by becoming an illustrator (or a designer). It is an accepted myth (even in most art schools) that real artists do not make money, but through accepting illustration into one's life comes the potential to earn a reasonable living while continuing to make art (or a reasonable substitute for art). Well, that paradigm has changed over the past dozen years. Art increasingly intersects with commerce, and artists have found that their muse-driven concepts can, under the right circumstances, be transformed into marketable products.

Likewise, illustrators have found that certain styles and conceptual trends are currently accepted as art in the hollowed halls of galleries, museums, and art fairs (like Art Basel). As sacrosanct distinctions are routinely challenged and with the boundaries between fine and applied arts becoming increasingly fungible, making a living (or at least somehow profiting) from art is not as difficult as it once was.

Of course, not all fine artists have the entrepreneurial gene, and not all illustrators are perfectly suited to perform in the art world, but for those who can make the respective leaps on either side of the divide, a potentially vital and welcoming market awaits. For the artist, it is a way to reach more of an audience with an alternative kind of "multiple"; for the illustrator, it is a way to branch out from the conventional problem/solution model into more self-initiated projects. But this is not an either/ or scenario. Illustrators are not required to become fine artists in order to expand their earning capabilities. In fact, the definitions of illustrator and of illustration are changing in such a way that editorial and advertising are no longer the only options. Illustrators are now able to show their work in art venues, just as more traditional artists are welcome in commercial venues.

The reason for this change is that, in the late twentieth and early twenty-first centuries, art has expanded to fill the many containers built with new technologies, economies, and moralities. Art is not restricted to canvas, clay, or paper and is as much a response to external media and mediums as it is to internal emotions. Moreover, the creative act is not determined by the ratio of suffering or angst to ultimate result, it is defined by the impulse to create something that has not existed before or build on something that has.

The consequence of this impulse is that artists and illustrators are currently creating "stuff." Not only are the boundaries between fine and applied arts more or less lowered, but form, content, and accessibility are more democratic. In this way, the entrepreneurial spirit is ignited, and graphically, greater options are now available. Below are some of the ways illustrative image-making has become more entrepreneurial.

Toys

With the explosion in vinyl toy marketing and manufacture with companies like Kidrobot and Giant Robot, illustrators have a new venue for their more absurdist, three-dimensional concepts. What began a decade ago with a few artists transforming action hero toys into mutations has grown into a highly profitable collectible industry.

Games

To say video games are a mammoth industry is not an exaggeration. Billions are spent annually on both development and sales, and illustrators are increasingly employed in rendering and development. While it is not always easy to create characters from scratch, the video game field welcomes as much creative thinking as it can absorb.

Animation

The most significant change in field of illustration can be summed up with the word *motion*. While illustrators have worked in the animation field since the first animated cartoons in the early twentieth century, digital technology allows anyone with software skills to be a desktop animator. Motion has become as common to illustrators as cross-hatching, and animation is now second nature.

Novelties

Illustrators have long toyed with the idea of creating knick-knacks, and some have produced delightful novelties that end up being sold in design-centric boutiques. They range from silly to profound, and they can be pure designs or concept- or character-driven.

Candies

This may not be the most prodigious of the entrepreneurial ventures, but specialty companies like Blue Q in Pittsfield, Massachusetts, produce various confections packaged with silly but cleverly illustrated covers and labels. Some artists have used their packaging skills to create custom lines of candy, as well.

Books

This is not an unconventional alternative, but increasingly, illustrators are turning to writing, illustrating, producing, and packaging books—and 'zines—that have independent life in the marketplace.

Graphic Novels

They are technically books, but graphic novels and artist books have a distinct genre of expression. Various specialty publishers, like *Drawn and Quarterly* and *Fantagraphics*, offer prodigious outputs of historical and original material, which increases the market for interesting new work.

Wallpaper

When it comes to products created by illustrators, the quirkier, the better; and few things are more unusual than wallpapers. While there is not an immense market for it, artists have, in recent years, become involved in wallpaper production, as well as designing wrapping paper and textiles.

Fashions

Speaking of textiles, designers have contributed their fair share to this field. But artists are increasingly developing all manner of clothing, from hats to shoes, and these days, hoodies.

T-shirts

A decade or so ago, when illustrators had an entrepreneurial inkling, their first thought was, Let's create a T-shirt line. The artful (and often just plain goofy) T-shirt industry has grown exponentially. It is also a good jumping-off point for other street fashion concepts.

A word to the wise: Illustration is a stepping stone, not an end in itself. Working with images opens doors to the above—and doubtless many other—unheralded jobs and genres. The key is to think entrepreneurially and to spread your talent as far as it will go.

The New Geppettos: Illustrators as Toy Makers

The prodigious and financially lucrative trend in eccentric, alternative toy objects, started over a decade ago in Japan, and with Tsunami force, washed over the United States and Europe. The phenomenon seemed so genuinely novel (in a post-punk, new-wave techno sort of way) that in some circles, these toys have come to define a twenty-first-century pop-cultural zeitgeist. They have certainly become an expressive medium for the many artists and illustrators bereft of traditional editorial and advertising outlets, and they appear to be a logical offshoot of new-wave animation and graphic novels.

The current wave of artist toys made by poster artists, graphic designers, and comic book makers—including Frank Kozik, Geoff McFettridge, Gary Baseman, and Tim Biskup, among others—are pushing limits of a different sort. Their work, which appears in alternative mags like *Juxtapoz*, is a fervent return to what might best be described as a consuming passion. Unlike their modernist forebears, the new toy producers are less concerned with making one-offs than they are with producing collectibles designed to feed their creative urges and simultaneously satisfy the desires of their acquisitive audience. Whereas the modernists agitatedly broke artistic conventions, the new generation feverishly rejects the typical mass-market toy models that they grew up with, but injects new concepts, materials, and most importantly, new mass-production techniques, into this otherwise venerable practice.

These new toy designers are filling a vacuum among sophisticated toy freaks who are not interested in mundane, licensed comic and film character action figurines (even the eccentric ones designed as movie tie-ins by the likes of filmmaker Tim Burton), and are appealing to the aesthetic needs of people like me who never bought action figures, but enjoy the design and tactility of these enticingly odd products. Although the main difference between the new art toys and old licensed versions (i.e., Power Rangers, Transformers, G.I. Joe) is their psychotic, post-Pokémon look, they nonetheless have similar marketing goals: Both are produced to be sold in quantity and both are intended to attract followings. Marketing aside, however, these new art toys have something else going for them: attitude. The new plastic, plush, and vinyl toys are more like iconic statuary. They are not actually meant to be played with, but rather displayed (and kept in their smartly designed packages). Making a physical object is the key. What's more, many exude a fetishistic quality, akin to the American Southwest native Hopi Kachina dolls, which have indirectly influenced many of the new toy makers.

So how have artist toys evolved from the one-offs of the modernists to the multiple characters of the postmodernists? How do they keep from falling into the traps of mainstream toy land? And why is there a common aesthetic that pervades the field and is imbued in even the most outré of these toys?

In the following interviews with the new Geppettos (including two pioneers from the early "new" toy movement, the founder of one of the leading toy emporiums, and three contemporary toymakers), we are given insight into their creative strategies.

David Kirk is the creator of the successful children's book series *Miss Spider's Tea Party*. In the late-1980s he sold his handmade wooden toys out of a storefront in New York's East Village.

In the '80s, you made and sold exquisite wooden toys: faces as banks with mouths that opened up to accept the money, and stacking toys, including a skeleton made of rings. How do you feel about the new toy makers' vinyl and plastic work?

The little plastic figures seem a slightly different area from what I used to do. For one thing, they appear to be part of a movement. There are lots of folks doing similar little beasties made just for today's collector. It's a little bit like those gilt-edged plates with pictures of dead movie stars that grandma hangs next to the cupboard with her best china, only this stuff is for guys in their teens and twenties.

They are a little too grotesque to sit next to the china. How do you feel about the art brut or grotesque aesthetic?

I did my share of deliberately ugly toys, but I usually like to concentrate more on what I think is beautiful or just fun. The current grotesque stuff is probably beautiful and fun for the artists who make it and for the collectors who buy it, so I'm all for it.

Your toys were so exquisitely crafted. Do think your stuff is passé?

For one thing, wouldn't that sort of toy-making have to have been big at some point in order for it to become passé? Maybe I don't get out enough, but I've never seen anybody at any point making toys with a combination of art and mechanics similar to my method. I don't think I was part of a time, or even ahead of my time. I was just a fluke with an odd skill set.

Why did you start making toys?

Because of my love of the toy robots I have collected since I was two. They broke a lot, and I had to take them apart to repair them, so I got to understand all sorts of simple mechanical systems. In high school, when I got seriously interested in art, I was fascinated by creepy things, like pain, squalor and death, as well as beautiful things like flowers and pretty girls. I got to be good at painting all those subjects, so when I made my toys, it was natural for me to make both cute animals and ugly monsters, both sexy dancing girls and spooky waltzing skeletons.

Who did you design toys for?

They weren't designed for adults or kids—they were designed for me.

Byron Glaser, with **Sandra Higashi**, invented Zolo (the postmodern Mr. Potato Head) and the first of the new wave of artist/designer toys.

What inspired you and Sandra Higashi to create Zolo?

We were working on the interior graphics for the FAO Schwarz flagship store on Fifth Avenue in New York City. [We] started to look at the toys that were being offered, and we both thought that there were some really big holes in the market.

Did you love toys as a child?

They have always played a part in our lives. Sandra was very good to her toys and still has some of them. I was much harder on mine.

How did Zolo reflect this passion?

With Zolo, we wanted to make a toy that inspired creativity and engaged whoever was playing with it. We wanted a toy that we would like to have. That was an element that was often missing for us in a lot of the toys that we were seeing around us. We wanted it to be loads of fun but to also inspire a message: that all kinds of shapes, colors, and patterns can work together and that the results can be extraordinary. At first, Zolo was only hand-carved out of wood. We thought as we were creating it that it also should reflect nature, which we are both in awe of. But it was not indestructible, as are so many toys today, so it was another good lesson for everyone playing with it to learn.

Did you use Mr. Potato Head as a model for Zolo?

Of course we both had the whole family of Potato Heads, but Mr. Potato Head is always a Mr., always a potato, always a head. I really don't think we had him in mind when we were creating Zolo. It was more about free-form and organic structure. Because many of the sculptures that you could make had animal-like characteristics, eyes became a part of it, but they were secondary elements. No offense to the Potato family, but that was the kind of one-note play pattern that we wanted to avoid.

Was there a style you were after? It looks very postmodern (like Memphis).

I think that is what appealed to the Museum of Modern Art in New York, where Zolo was first sold exclusively through its trade sales division. Actually, it rejects a rigid genre distinction. No one knew where Zolo should belong on the shelf. Was it for boys or girls? Should it go in 'construction' or would it fit better in 'arts and crafts'? A few years ago, the toy industry recognized Zolo as creating a new category—we called it 'playsculpture.' Before, Zolo toys were positioned for either boys or girls. Now there are lots of toys that are for both. One of our favorite response cards came from a woman in her nineties who suffered from arthritis. She played with [Zolo] every day because it made her feel creative and it was good for her hands. Like postmodernism, Zolo rejects the boundaries between high and low forms of art. It is also about playfulness. I think there was a lot going on in the culture at that time that is reflected in Zolo. Maybe it's the patterns that feel like Memphis, but people have said it reminds them of Miro, too. Part of the appeal of Zolo is that it often reminds people of something. I think it more closely resembles the inside of Sandra's wardrobe.

Was Zolo originally meant for commercial application?

We weren't really thinking about that. We were thinking it was fun and we wanted it, so we thought other people would want it too, and of course children would like it. We had no idea how the toy industry was structured at that time. The only way we were going to see it [sold] at FAO Schwarz was if we were going to make it ourselves. While Zolo was [on sale] at the MoMa, it made up a third of their trade sales. We were not really prepared to handle those kinds of numbers, so we had to learn quickly. Not that it has ever become easy for us.

Where is the product these days?

We sell Zolo 5, the fifth generation of the handmade wooden sets. Of course, they all work together, so people who have all five sets can really go to town. This set has metal studs, feathers, silver leaf, and fuzzy balls. We are also in production for a new plastic set that has mixed materials as well; it's more affordable and is a game. We also have a line of anatomically incorrect Bonz with movable joints that you can build with, [which] we license to Curious Pictures in New York.

Are you involved in the new generation of vinyl toys?

We love the category and the medium. We always try to keep Zolo interactive and not necessarily iconic, which a lot of the vinyl tends to be. Maybe someday that will feel appropriate for Zolo. I would love for that to happen.

Paul Budnitz is an entrepreneur. He is founder of Kidrobot and creator of MUNNY, a tabula rasa toy to which many artists contribute.

What is the most important trait to look for when selecting an artist to create a toy?

The design itself. Kidrobot is not about working with well-known or famous artists (although we do). We are about the very best design. So if someone sends us an amazing design, we'll make it. Personally, I look for designs that are flat, feel new, *and are unique. I have a sign over my office that says 'nostalgia is death,' and that is basically our creative philosophy. We choose to look forward, not backwards.*

How much of Kidrobot's toy design is art versus commerce? Do the two coexist easily?

It is all art and it is all commerce. As far as I'm concerned there is no conflict whatsoever, and this is not a distinction that I tend to make. Shakespeare wrote his plays for money; if he didn't perform, he didn't eat. Any fine artist who tells you he doesn't care about money is probably lying to you. There is a famous story about Picasso and Brecht: Brecht wanted to make a lot of money so he could pass it down to his children, so he collected Picasso. Picasso wanted a lot of money so he could pass it down to his children, and he also collected Picasso.

As more and more artists' toys hit the market, what makes your biggest "invention," MUNNY, so unique?

MUNNY is just really great design. The body shape, the accessories, and the spirit of this toy are what make it special. I don't think this is something that can be copied or imitated.

Now that these toys, and Kidrobot in particular, have found a hungry market, what's to stop Kidrobot from becoming the next Mattel?

You mean what stops Kidrobot from becoming a giant conglomerate that makes essentially lifeless, joyless toys that crush children's creative spirit?

I stop that from happening because I can't imagine why I'd be interested in doing it. Our customers and fans also stop us from doing it, because if we did, they'd abandon us, and I'd be out there encouraging them.

Tim Biskup is a cartoonist, lettering artist, sculptor, and creator of Gama-Go clothing and gift items. He is founder of the Bispop Gallery in Pasadena, California, where he exhibits and sells original paintings, hand-painted objects, clothing, toys, books, cards, and exclusive items.

Why did you start designing toys?

I've been into toys my whole life. All of my work is inspired by toys. About eight years ago, I started to collect Japanese monster toys. The colors, shapes, and general feeling of them made a huge impact on me and really changed my art. I dreamed about making my own, but it never seemed possible. The learning curve, the set-up expense, marketing—all of that just seemed too much to deal with. Then I was approached by Sony Creative to design a set of PVC figures. I was totally blown away that I was actually going to get something made. After that, it was a snowball effect. I got offers from five or six other companies that wanted to make my toys before the Sony toys ever got made. I just went nuts.

Who were your other influences?

As a kid I loved building toys, like Lego, Lincoln Logs, and Tinker Toys. I'm interested in making toys that bridge the gap between the collectible objects that sit on your desk and the toys that inspire people to pick them up and play with them. Kaiju toys were really the big thing for me around the time that I started making my own, but there are tons of earlier influences that I've started to tap into.

Did you really think you'd find a market?

By the time I started making toys there was already enough of a market that I knew I could sell through some small editions. I am always a little freaked out when I do something that doesn't fit into the market that I know. I'm working on some projects that are a big step away from the format and price range that most toy collectors are used to. I'm a little nervous about it.

Could you have imagined that the market would become as large as it has for Kidrobot and other alternative toy stores?

Not at all. I'm stunned that it has gone as crazy as it has.

What is the single most significant theme of your toys?

It's tough to find a single theme because I feel like I have two distinctly different themes that exist in various combinations in my toys. The first is modular design. I want the toys to be inviting and interactive. The other theme is an attempt to find balance. I try to combine ugliness and beauty, cuteness and malevolence, happiness and sadness.

Are they for kids or adults or what?

Ideally they're for both kids and adults. Most of the art that I like—from Looney Tunes to Jean Tinguely—appeals to both groups. There is a big divide in most people's minds about enjoying something in a very playful, childlike way and enjoying it in an observant, intellectual way. I do whatever I can to remind myself of what I liked as a kid and try to incorporate that into my work. There is something very satisfying about diving into one of those big pools of plastic balls. They should have those for adults. Hey, I should make one of those for adults!

Have you limited yourself to a certain niche of characters or are you branching out?

I hope I never limit myself like that. I try really hard to keep myself fresh and not rely on a character to carry an idea. I do use a few characters over and over, but only when I feel that it works in the context of the piece. I also try to make a point of letting characters change over time and from one piece to another. There's really no right way to draw any of them. It's important not to define characters too clearly. I don't want to be too much of a storyteller. I'm always branching out. There are so many characters in my art that I feel like I can keep going forever. The little freaky bug in the corner of some painting could easily be a little figure next week.

Who is your favorite toy maker?

A Japanese company called M-Ichigo (or M-I).

Gary Baseman is an artist, TV and movie producer, toy designer, and prolific cartoonist. He is the creator of the the critically acclaimed animated television series *Teacher's Pet* and the feature-length film of the same name.

Why did you start designing toys?

I have always had an interest since I [began collecting] vintage toys, along with anything that I feel are little works of art. I truly see these toys as limited-edition sculptures for the masses.

You show in retail stores and galleries. Isn't there a conflict?

My goal really is to blur the lines between fine art and toy culture. I am honored that the Laguna Art Museum is exhibiting the toys and paintings together in a two-man show, Perversion: The Art of Gary Baseman and Tim Biskup. *(summer 2006). I love how [people] can enjoy the art in the museum, then step over to the store and buy their own little work of art.*

How did you actually begin making toys?

I was traveling in Japan for a collaborative three-man show with Mark Ryden and Tim Biskup. In Tokyo, I was invited by Sony Creative to produce the set of five vinyl figures that turned into my original Dunce series. I originally used a dunce icon in my paintings as a metaphor of man being a fool for love. I turned the series into the Obedience School Dropouts, with characters like Re-Tardy, whose offense is that he is always late.

Were there any previous influences, for example, David Kirk or some of the earlier wood toy makers?

I love David Kirk's original wood toys. They are beautiful and I own a few. But a true work of art that inspired me in vinyl was KAWS original black companion. It is a skull head on a Mickey Mouse body that I first saw in SoHo in the New Museum window. I also love the feel of composition; how they look and how they feel. One of my goals is to find a way to recreate the process for my own sculptures. I have many old mannequin heads and hands, along with old wood-jointed toys such as Felix the Cat and Pete the Pup.

You must have been steeped in Japanese aesthetics.

Yes, the Japanese sensibility plays a role too, especially the Kaiju toys produced in the 1950s and 1960s. I am also inspired by Murakami and Nara, who know how to blur the lines between fine art and toy culture very well.

How did you imagine you would sell your toys in the beginning?

I did not imagine anything. Then again, I imagine everything. I have always wanted to take over the universe by creating special things.

What is the single most significant theme of your toys?

The themes of my toys are no different from the themes of my art, which are desire, longing, and control.

Are they for kids or adults or yourself?

For myself! I don't delineate who they are for. I guess you would say adults. My art is for adults. But kids can take a simpler theme away with them because my work mixes popular culture and surrealism and looks like cartoons. The Fire Water Bunnies are the only exception, because they were created for children.

They were created originally for a Taiwanese folklore water festival. Dumb Luck the rabbit was based on a gallery show at the Mendenhall Gallery in Los Angeles in 1999. Toby, a plush, was created for my For the Love of Toby gallery show at Billy Shire Fine Arts, which included 80 works of art. Toby was created to be a best friend, a mirror, a shadow, somebody who knows all your dirty little secrets but loves you unconditionally. I wanted him to be plush so you could take him to bed.

Have you limited yourself to a certain niche of characters?

Limit? What does that mean? The goal is always to [screw] around and take risks and grow; try new material, new characters. Anything to try to discover little human truths. Anything to keep my mind off my miserable life.

Who is your favorite toy maker?

My favorite has been Conor Libby at Critterbox because of his attention to detail. But I will be working with a lot of other cool toy makers, too. Medicom has produced amazing work. I have done Hump QEE with Raymond at Toy2R, [which] I love—the new Gold Egg is amazing.

Geoff McFetridge is a graphic designer, animator, filmmaker, and all-around "visual auteur." McFetridge created the opening title sequences for the movies *Adaptation* and *The Virgin Suicides.* He is founder of Champion Graphics.

What prompted you to make artist toys?

I resisted for a while, since I was not very involved in the toy world. I was given toys over time but never collected them. It is such an interesting culture, though. I decided that as an outsider, maybe I could do something interesting and different.

Do you always have an audience in mind, or are the toys extensions of your expressive needs?

Most of the design is pretty autobiographical. I try to have the designs be part of visual discussion, so that they speak on a level that the viewer understands, like a little conversation.

How often do you develop a new toy or series of toys?

Not often.

Are they for children or all of us?

My daughter liked them for about a day. They are also a choking hazard. I would have liked them when I was a kid, I think.

In your universe, fundamentally, what makes something a toy?

Smallish, pointless, and dimensional.

Maira Kalman: Illustrator? Author? Dilettante?

Maira Kalman is an illustrator as author, author as illustrator, author as designer, and designer as entrepreneur. The creator of children's books and museum products, she does not rely on a single genre or medium to satisfy her creative needs.

Did you set out to be an illustrator?

My first inkling of art was to be a writer. I had visions of sitting in a quiet country room, looking out into a garden, writing. Something happened. I could not stand my writing. It was too serious; too laden with heavy idiocy. I thought drawing would be a refreshing pastime, not a serious endeavor. And maybe that lack of seriousness allowed me to experiment and to find out something about drawing.

Would you refer to yourself as an illustrator? And if not, what?

Maybe illustrator explains part of it. Maybe an author as well. Maybe dilettante.

Why did you select children's books as your first foray into the field?

I wanted to write and paint and I was not sure how to do that. Then some things became clearer. Alice in Wonderland *is the greatest children's book ever written, and it stunned me. And then Ludwig Bemelmans wrote for adults and children. And then Kay Thompson wrote without any punctuation whatsoever, and maybe her audience was not just children. And then* Wind in the Willows *blew into my life. And* Pippi Longstocking. *I thought the best children's books were good for all audiences. And then I could be smart and stupid. Long and short. Sad and merry. There were no limits of approach.*

You've done editorial and advertising, and you even had a visual column on the *New York Times* Web site. Do you have a favorite métier?

The New York Times *was my most beloved project to date. Some odd chemistry, some odd atmosphere of wondering and wandering allowed me to speak and paint my mind.*

Aside from traveling all over the place, how much of your day is spent making things?

It would be nice if the entire day were made up of making things. I consider washing dishes important time. And making the bed is very important time. So I am making things all day long, even if it is only making beds.

So would it be more accurate to call you a maker of things than an illustrator?

You predicted the answer to your previous question. That is a lovely way to look at how I spend my day. I don't want to know the difference between work and life.

Your work is all about telling stories. What triggers a particular story? Is it observation? Autobiography? Serendipity?

All of the above. Some force allows the brain to engage these different aspects and they combine in some misty way. It is amazing how often you have no idea why something came to you, or why a particular vision of a perplexed woman wearing a green hat evokes such a strong response. I don't question the sources, I just accept the fact. And then there is longing: for what, I don't know. Peace of mind, perhaps, with a spritz of interest.

In the beginning there was a primitive quality to your work. How do you feel you've evolved?

Somehow I have learned to be a better painter. I don't know if that is good yet. It is elusive.

So much of your work is about color. What does color mean to you?

Usually I like things that are white, so I don't know why I am so colorful in my paintings. And I don't like to think I am overly colorful or garish. What are colors? They are memories of a time and place and light and breeze. And they are very concrete and stabilizing.

This book is about alternatives to (and the future of) illustration. You've done many alternatives. What is next?

Besides wanting to be a maid for the Duchess of Devonshire, I would like to:

1. *Walk around the world (or some nice, gentle, green part of it)*
2. *Perform in some Tanztheater event, though I am getting older and the likelihood of that is really slim*
3. *Run a small store and sell things that I and other people make*
4. *Spend more time sitting in gardens, drawing, reading, or embroidering*
5. *Collaborate with my children on various projects*
6. *Get rid of excessive possessions*
7. *Not speak for good amounts of time*

Richard McGuire's Animated Expressionism

Fear(s) of the Dark is a collection of five animations by five international artists— Charles Burns, Lorenzo Mattotti, Marie Cailllou, Blutch, and Pierre Di Sciullo— linked by two demonstrative conceits. Each piece is produced in black and white (with the occasional red accent), and each addresses an atavistic, nightmarish fear. Although uneven in spots, the film is a tour de force for its emotional intensity (it's amazing how much tension can be conveyed with brush and pen strokes). Among most fully realized in terms of technical mastery and narrative eloquence is the work of Richard McGuire. In addition to being a visual tale designed to provoke the ultimate fear, the film is a masterpiece of graphic erudition that must be seen to be fully appreciated. McGuire began as an illustrator and comic artist with ambitions for animated storytelling. The commission for this film was a shot of adrenaline. Fortunately, his visibility in major magazines gave his work the allure it needed to land the gig.

After what seems like many years, the feature film to which you have contributed a major section, *Fear(s) of the Dark,* was screened in New York City at the French Film Festival at Lincoln Center. What is the film all about?

The film is a meditation on fear; each artist designed and directed a story under that general theme. Some of the stories are inter-cut, some stand alone, and there is a collection of short pieces that recur throughout. Each segment seems to reflect the other in ways we didn't plan, primordial fears we all share.

Did artistic director Étienne Robial give you any specific directives as to your segment, or was this a blank slate?

The title and concept came from Prima Linea, the producers. The only limitation was that the film would be in black and white. No other directive was given. Étienne Robial designed the opening and closing credits and was involved in the sequencing of the parts. His involvement with bande dessinée artists goes back to his days with Futuropolis [the pioneering French comics publisher], which he co-founded.

What is the gist of your segment? What is your fear?

My segment, without giving away too much, is about a man confronting madness and the unexpected violence that can sometimes erupt from madness. That's the gist, but there are other fears interlaced. There are some direct quotes from nightmares I've had. I've always been a bit claustrophobic, so I've managed to work that in there as well. It's funny, I was just remembering, there's a scene in the film where a man is startled by a bat in a house. While we were working on that scene the same thing happened to me! I had visited some friends in the country. One late evening I went to my room, and suddenly there was this bat swooping down on me and circling around. After I managed to shoo it out the window, I made some notes and drawings to capture just how my body reacted.

Did you do much preparation to capture the essence of fear?

One of the things I did at the start of the project was to go back and look at all the films that had scared me and analyze what exactly made them work. In some cases it's purely sound; in a lot of cases it's what you don't see.

We are all afraid of the dark in some way. Did you do anything extraordinary to make your fear bigger than life?

In building the sound design, which is one of the parts of the process I love the most, you can play with layering some unexpected things into the mix to enhance a moment. For example, there is a scene where someone is locked in a closet and he is kicking the door to get out. We recorded the sound of a guy kicking a door, and although it was accurate it lacked the power I had imagined. It just wasn't big enough. I wanted something more booming, so we took the sound of muffled explosions and mixed them in to match each kick and then it felt right.

There are all sorts of subliminal things with the sound, like where someone walks though a door in a dream sequence, I added the sound of someone inhaling; the exhale sound happens only when the dream finishes. I think the held breath adds tension. You may not necessarily be aware of it because you are watching other things, but I think you feel it. Earlier in the same sequence a man gets a splinter in his hand, but because it is a dream I didn't want the sound to be completely realistic. We tried many different sounds for when he is pulling the splinter out, but we finally used an aggressive pull of a violin string and the slap sound it makes when it hits. This worked emotionally; it was such a physical sound, kind of violent and unexpected.

I decided to be spare with the music. I didn't want to use music in the conventional way. It's too easy to lay down some uncomfortable music to give the cue of what to feel. Sometimes music adds too much of a distance to what you are watching. I wanted it very quiet and intimate. I wanted bring the viewer as close to the action as I could.

Your work usually is, if not warm and cozy, at least not gothic or scary. Did you have to alter your visual style for the film?

It's one of the reasons I said yes to this project, to push myself. It was a challenge to create an experience for the audience to feel on an emotional level. That was the goal.

I didn't feel going in that I had a universe to protect the way most of the other artists did. Stylistically I think I'm pretty flexible. I was trying to find my solution to this particular situation. The film I made [before Fear(s) of the Dark] *looked nothing like this one. In that one (*Micro Loup*) everything is seen from above looking straight down for the entire film. Everything is abstracted, but once you realize what you're seeing, you follow the story logically.* Fear(s) *has another way of using abstraction, by putting so much in the dark. Some scenes are so minimal that you need the sound to complete the image, otherwise you're lost. In my research for designing the film I came across the work of Felix Vallotton, a Swiss artist from the turn of the century. In his graphic work he often did a trick of black on black, a person wearing black against a black background. I liked the way the mind would complete the image. I knew this was a key to how to approach the film.*

As I noted, you worked on this for a long time. What were your major hurdles? Why did it take so long?

Mostly every animated film takes years to make; it's a very slow process. It takes days, sometimes weeks, to make seconds. At the beginning we went down a few

18

wrong roads, the first one with the story itself. I chose a short story that I thought would work. It had some nice visuals but the ending wasn't great, and as I worked on the storyboard and tried to solve the end I got lost with it—it just wasn't satisfying. I nearly gave up completely after months of work. I showed a friend, Michel Prius, what I had done. He's a cartoonist and writer who has a history of collaborations behind him. We went through it all. I pointed out the things I liked, and then we brainstormed and transformed the story. Once that was in place, just finding the choice of technique took time. For the previous film I primarily used Flash. We thought we would do the same with this one, but it became obvious pretty quickly that it wasn't going to work. We looked into using 'motion-capture', we discussed the possibly of 3-D, but in the end we went with traditional hand-drawn animation, then combined it with Flash to ink and cleaned the drawings. Later, in some cases, we combined a few techniques. There were all sorts of technical problems that needed to be worked out. Sometimes it was hard to get the software to look integrated. Some backgrounds and objects were created in 3-D. After Effects was used to add a blur to the light from the candle.

Apropos of Valloton, it is very graphic and very dark...

The funny thing is, the way I designed the film, very little is really seen! For instance, we would design a room with all the furniture, rugs, and wallpaper, and then turn the lights out. A character is walking through the space but we only see the little area around the candle glow. Although we don't see much it all had to really be there in order to feel right.

Who is this film made for? I, for one, would rather forget my fears rather than see them before me on the silver screen.

Our film is not exactly a genre picture, but the subject has certainly attracted some of that audience. It also appeals to the comic audience, which is taken very seriously in France.

I was recently invited to a horror festival [that included] our film. It was very odd to watch a hardcore gore film with fans of the genre. It was more like an amusement ride than a film experience. I was very aware of being in an audience. They were vocal and were really participating with the film.

When I go to see a film, I want to get absorbed in what is going on in the story and lose myself to the experience. I can get excited by a psychological thriller or a good ghost story, but I'm not interested in anything with gratuitous violence.

Which of the segments most scares you?

My own, of course.

Todd Radom's Illustrated Sports Logos

Todd Radom had long been a sports fan, but that was not enough for him to land highly visible jobs designing sports graphics for major franchises. He had to convince clients he had the right stuff. His illustrations always leaned towards the iconic, a perfect technique for this kind of work. He created a focused portfolio, started attracting clients, and the rest followed suit.

How did you become a specialist in sports logos?

I've been a sports fan, specifically a big baseball fan, since I was a kid. I was always intrigued by uniform designs and logos, and explored these themes as a design student at the School of Visual Arts (SVA). My first jobs out of college were in the book publishing industry, designing trade jackets and covers. I probably designed more covers for baseball titles than just about anyone in the late '80s and early '90s. At this time I was branching off into advertising and corporate work, [doing] lots of logos. It seemed like a logical move for me to aggressively pitch my talent, knowledge, and passion as a sports fan and consumer to the professional sports leagues.

I got my first freelance commission from Major League Baseball in 1992. These days I have sort of a niche within the field of sports design as a historian. I am both a designer who can execute, and a guy who knows the history of sports and the history of sports design. I have compiled a very deep library of uniform and logo designs and histories over the years.

There is a definite tradition of convention with regard to the design of team brands. How do you balance your design with those conventions?

There is definitely a visual culture for professional sports in our country, and I think that the need to speak the consumer's language means that we have to live comfortably within those conventions. I personally try very hard to stay away from anything that smacks of trendiness. I want to create a package that will stand the test of time whether that time frame proves to be three years or twenty years. This is a tough concept to articulate verbally, but I like to think that my work, for the most part, has a carefully crafted, timeless quality.

20

As an aside: event logos are part of our world too—logos for Super Bowls, All Star Games, significant anniversaries, and the like. These are designs with a limited shelf life and [they] involve some dynamics that set them apart from permanent identity projects.

Like any other prominent consumer logo, these things go through focus groups and market testing. I have never knowingly had a creative director lay down a mandate that revolved around this kind of 'tail wagging the dog' approach, but consumers certainly expect something that appropriately lives within the visual culture of sports. Sports design relies upon the sale of licensed goods, especially apparel, to generate revenue, so it's incumbent upon me or anyone else doing this kind of work to consider the worlds of fashion and retail to some extent. The peculiarities and traditions of local markets are especially relevant.

A decade ago, the Washington Bullets changed their name for "social" reasons. What are the taboos—like racial or ethnic issues—in creating sports identities?

Goodwill is a critical component in trying to connect to the masses. We are trying to appeal to a broad swatch demographically, so the sensible concept of 'first, do no harm' is something that should be employed. Baseball has its Cleveland Indians, football has its Washington Redskins. The influence of sports on our culture is undeniable, even as our tortured national debate on race and ethnicity evolves.

What would you say is your most "experimental" logo?

I get called on for more or less traditionally-focused identities that project well into the present; I am all about ribbons, retro inspired typography, and symmetry. The identity that really evolved into something completely different for me would have to be the logo for the World Baseball Classic, an international event that forced me to channel my 'inner Paul Rand.'

There seems to be a trend in sports to at once return to the past and push to the future in terms of logos, uniforms, and even stadium design. Is this a valid observation?

Absolutely valid. Sports franchises provide comfort and continuity in a transient world. There's something very nice about the fact that the St. Louis Cardinals have employed two birds perched on a baseball bat as their visual identity since 1922. The two new baseball stadiums that will open here in New York next season are faithfully retro-based; I think it'll be very interesting to see what the public thinks about them in 25 years or so.

There was a trend toward aggressive and complex franchise identities in the early '90s, just as the Mac was becoming the designer's primary tool. I think that we have devolved in the years since—back to basics, back to comfort. Like so many trends, it seems that in sports the envelope is pushed far to the perimeter, then the pendulum swings back to a sensible and comfortable place. There are exceptions, of course—take a look at the Arizona Cardinals' striking modern stadium out in the desert, or the Washington Nationals' new urban (and LEED-certified) ballpark.

What are the extant logos today that you'd like to see changed, and why?

I would have to start with the NFL's Detroit Lions. Most people don't realize that most current NFL logos and helmet designs only date back to the early 1960s, when the great marriage of professional football and television necessitated decorated helmets. The Lions' identity, which was tweaked a few years back, isn't rooted in grand tradition like the Packers' simple 'G.' This is a franchise that has won only one playoff game since 1957, playing in a city that has gone through decades of turbulence and social upheaval. It would seem to me that the timing is perfect for a new identity.

What are the logos that should never change?

The Montréal Canadiens' visual identity is so integral to the distinct culture of French-speaking Canada that I think it deserves special status. The Yankees' interlocking 'NY' connects generations of great teams and fans (and I'm a diehard Red Sox fan, so I must appreciate what it represents). The Yankees actually employ two distinct 'NYs,' one on their uniform and one on their cap. (By the way, the ligature was designed by Louis B. Tiffany in 1877 as part of the first New York City Police Medal of Honor. The award was presented to Patrolman John McDowell, who was shot and wounded in the line of duty; the ball club adopted the emblem in 1909.)

Animating Animation with J.J. Sedelmaier

Sedelmaier is a lifelong fan of illustration. He's devoted the better part of his professional life to making drawings move and tell a story. The firm bearing his name has done some of the great pop culture animations with a score of illustrators, some who had never done animation before.

You run an animation studio and employ a lot of illustrators. What determines who you will use?

It's always dictated by the concept. I cast the projects I do by choosing not only the design source, but the animator and sound design as well. It's always the mixture of these elements and their relationship that makes for a successful 'soup.'

You've been doing this for some time. Has the market for illustrators doing motion gotten larger or smaller?

If you had asked me last year I'd have said it's gotten smaller, but it's recently moved towards using illustrators again. I can theorize that this is due to computer-generated imagery (CGI) plateauing in terms of growth, and the fact that there's been enough time for the CGI technique to show its limitations. People are realizing that there's a human quality to hand-drawn work that adds warmth and humanity to certain types of animation. This goes back to that balance I mentioned earlier. But digital technology also provides opportunities. Many designers have a style that's computer-friendly in a graphic sense, and their style is, as a result, translated more faithfully to film. All this adds up to more use of illustrators, I guess.

Do you foresee a saturation point where the kind of animation you do will be less in demand than it is now?

No, I don't think so. Fact is, we use computer/digital technology (and have since 1991), but our work doesn't brand itself by graphic technique. Animation is so much more than any one style. We're pretty nimble and our reputation is rooted in flexibility and versatile approaches. As long as the ideas we produce using film differ from one another, we should be able to dwell in the industry a bit longer.

The other aspect of running a business like this is to stay as small as you can and not succumb to fads. We stay out of the long-form world so that we can continue to produce variety. I love the fact that if you Google us you'll probably get awfully confused. (Animation, gay/lesbian, railroads, architectural preservation/ restoration, comic books, etc.)

With all the slick Pixar-style animation, do you see illustrators becoming more computer savvy?

Sure, but is that because of the 'slick Pixar animation' or because computers are the tool of the hour? The computer, and a paperless approach to design production, are simply facts of life. I learned to draw with pencils and love the feel of the lead dragging across the tooth of the paper. Isn't that sweet? But it doesn't mean it's better, it's just another tool. How can you grow up today and not be computer savvy? Maybe to someone my age it's 'savvy,' but to most people younger than me it is a no-brainer. I guess I'm pencil savvy, car savvy, and telephone (rotary) savvy.

What is more important in selecting illustrators, their technique or their conceptual ability?

Both. And I'd hope the two are inseparable. I think this applies to whether the artist is alive or dead.

Since the days of Ren and Stimpy, animated cartoons have been much more raw in tone and style. Is this the past, present, or future?

*This is the present taking the past and making it the future. John Kricfalusi took the classic cartoon of the past and rocketed it into our face—in fact, it's still careening off the walls! But he wasn't the first to do it; there was a foundation laid by his mentor and major influence, Bob Clampett. You also have to give credit to folks like Jay Ward and Bill Scott (*Rocky and Bullwinkle*), Richard Williams (*Roger Rabbit*), Matt Groening (*The Simpsons*), and, frankly, all the short network IDs that MTV was doing. Traditional animation (cel, 2-D, etc.) is now almost exclusively for adults.* Family Guy, *[the animated segments on]* SNL, South Park, The Simpsons, *and even* SpongeBob SquarePants, *are all steeped in parody. You couldn't say that until recently.*

If an artist/illustrator wants to do animation, what must he or she do?

Lose a major lobe of [his or her] brain? Study film, not just animation, and if possible, teach yourself or take very generic courses so you don't get distracted by someone else's (or another studio's) technique. I love the animation work of artists like Jonathon Rosen. He learned the technology and made films that are so purely his vision—it's very exciting! You can also associate yourself with a studio whose work you like or you feel you are in good hands with. Just don't forget that your personal spin on design can be just as unique in another medium as long as you look at the opportunities freshly. Make it your own!

Making Characters: The Pictoplasma Phenomenon

Certain illustrators are maestros of complexity, while others revel in simplicity. Both are real virtues, but in the world of punchy icons—a breed of illustration that has picked up steam since the advent of the computer and is currently one of the most frequently practiced—simplicity is truly essential. The graphic icon is the total opposite of the graphic poster. While a poster must be seen from ten feet away (a distance that makes it equivalent to the size of a computer icon), an icon must carry a visual wallop usually from ten (or fewer) inches away and at less than a half-inch square or circumference. Some are larger, but small is the norm.

The illustrated character business is so "hot" these days that Pictoplasma—a Berlin-based publisher of books and online resources devoted to contemporary comic, illustrative, and graphic icons—sponsored a conference in New York City in 2008 devoted to "Contemporary Character Design and Art." It was a gathering place for a diverse crowd of artists, designers, animators, and producers to freely exchange ideas about anything and everything related to character design.

Besides presentations, lectures, and panels, Pictoplasma's animation screenings explored how graphical characters previously not associated with the industry are taking the medium by storm. There's a market out there for this stuff.

We asked Peter Thaler of Pictoplasma to discuss this current trend.

What exactly is the Pictoplasma phenomenon?

Pictoplasma was founded at the end of 1999, to serve as a first-ever platform for an extensive collection and archive of contemporary character design. As a reaction to the overwhelming flood of iconographic figures on Web sites, billboards, and food packaging, the project wanted to set a considered, stylistically sure-footed, high-quality collection of figures against the daily glut of random mascots and pathetic sympathy seekers. From the beginning, Pictoplasma's main goal has been to free character representation from commercial intentions and the popular psychology of story telling while linking a new breed of character design to the birth of a graphical language beyond all cultural boundaries. Meanwhile, the project has developed into a lively platform and has published numerous books and DVDs on the topic. Pictoplasma organizes annual conferences and festivals, curates exhibitions, and has closely accompanied the scene as it moves toward a completely new understanding of characters.

25

As we started the project at the turn of the century, a global scene of character designers was producing milliards of happy DJ depictions. Cute and cuddly robots were far removed from feelings of technological paranoia.

Naïve boys and girls with over-the-top expressions and ecstatically widened pupils promised a bright future. Just three years later, the same golden boys and girls were tortured, twisted, and mutilated. The blunt combination of cute and abused, naïve and sexualized, harmless and violent became the focus of content. Today things seem to have changed again. Suddenly characters are now being brought into a personal, almost spiritual, and even religious context. They are born, grow up, make mistakes, replicate, grow old, eventually die, and either go to heaven or hell—or they are simply reincarnated. What struck us during the research for our latest compilation publication, The Character Encyclopedia, *was the vast amount of previously unseen characters exhaling their anthropomorphic souls in the moment of death. We're pretty sure that the creators weren't aware that there were uncountable other artists around the world drawing on the exact same motif.*

By collecting, de-contextualizing, and comparing the work of a global scene of artists, designers, illustrators, and animators, we are trying to examine the artistic, referential, and contextual developments of the current generations populating our character universe.

How did this passion for creating icons come about?

It was around the turn of the millennium that we saw the emergence of character design on a new level via the Internet. Much of character design is rooted in game design and pixel characters. Working with pixels and the Net requires simplicity of form. Characters need to be small and communicable. So contemporary characters are just visuals, not unlike empty screens. They function as letters, typography, and ideograms.

At the start, we generally related more to these reduced and abstract designs than to arabesque and detailed or naturalistic illustrations. But by now we get excited about some new artist doing collages, super detailed vector work, or cut outs, installations, [or] extremely rough, spontaneous pencil scribbles.

Is it purely a function of the computer or is there another ancestry?

Being so visually pared-down, characters are highly effective in the media-driven world. Their global dissemination owes much to the Internet, which imposes its own technical limitations on the design. From the perspective of media theory, characters are the inscription of the Internet medium. And their message is that of the Internet itself: the phantasm of global contact and communication. eBoy's strategy of digitizing the world pixel by pixel might be interpreted along these lines.

But the impact of character design is not limited to digital media.

From a broader point of view, character design is a contemporary graphical language. It functions as a thesaurus for the transmission of meaning beyond alphabetical syntax. Similar to the logic of the logo, character design operates through abstraction, metaphoric density, and a play with visiotypes. In this way, characters reach adults and children alike, breeding their own audience in the phenomenon of 'kidult'—the generation that refuses to grow up.

Who are the leaders of this movement?

Depending on what field you are looking at—design, illustration, animation, street or fine art—there are many established and upcoming artists worth mentioning. In the fields of high and fine art, many contemporary superstars are using reduced and abstract character visuals in their work. The famous Japanese artists Takashi Murakami and Yoshitomo Nara, but also others such as the American Paul McCartney or the Chapman Brothers, are working with the same repeating characters and a very distinct and reduced style.

Many character designers are referencing art that could be contextualized in the tradition of surrealism, dilettante [art], and pop art. They play with an array of forms from our cultural imagery, both from popular and archaic culture, and transform them to their own families of characters. The evolving systems suggest a world of their own, a kind of pop-sur-reality after the so-called hyper-reality propagated in the 1990s. The most distinct artists working in such a way are Boris Hoppek (GER), Friends With You (USA), and Doma (ARG). Currently we are witnessing an exciting revival of dilettante art and neo-folklore from up-and-coming, talented artists such as Shoboshobo (FR), Dennis Tyfus (BE), AJ Fossik, and Dylan Martorell (AUS).

What would you say are the most successful images (what is required)?

The key to character design is investing the design with an appearance of life, an anthropomorphic appeal—animating it in the sense of lending it an 'anima,' or soul. It is what we project onto the image that triggers this animation, but it is the density and strength of the design that makes a character an ideal screen for our imaginations, so we have the impression that what we see is looking back at us. Many artists and designers in contemporary character design play with this dichotomy of incorporation and animation versus lifelessness. In digital images, again, every highlight sparkling in the character's eyes reinforces the absence of a real life. The industrial sterility of urban collector toys and the charm of plush dolls are other attempts to escape two-dimensionality. Behind all these strategies lies the graphical quality of the character, making its powerful emotional connection with the viewer.

How can an artist / illustrator break into the form?

By making a powerful emotional connection with the viewer.

Chapter Two

The Illustrator as Storyteller:
A Story by Marshall Arisman

Historically, the lifeblood of the illustrator required that the work be printed. As a result, publishing was limited to the illustrators chosen by art directors to appear in national magazines. The illustrations rarely stood alone without assigned text. Now, once the illustrator connects to the Internet, personal stories, accompanied by the user's illustrations, are at once global and free. No longer relying upon the publishing industry, the illustrator as storyteller can explore personal vision without an art director's or editor's permission.

The individual with the capacity to write and illustrate is no longer at the mercy of the large corporation for exposure. Self-publishing is now an option for all who have something to say about themselves and about the world that surrounds them.

Clay Shirky, in his wonderful book *Here Comes Everybody* (The Penguin Press, 2008), states, "In a world where publishing is effortless, the decision to publish something isn't terribly momentous. Just as movable type raised the value of being able to read and write even as it destroyed the scribal tradition, globally free publishing is making public speech and action more valuable, even as its absolute abundance diminishes the specialness of professional publishing. For a generation that is growing up without the scarcity that made publishing such a serious pursuit, the written word has no special value in and of itself. Adam Smith, in *The Wealth of Nations*, pointed out that although "water is far more important than diamonds to human life, diamonds are far more expensive, because they are rare."

It is not rare that illustrators are trained in the figurative art of drawing and painting. What is rare—but not for long—is the understanding that personal stories can become the platform for illustrated text.

YouTube, MySpace, and numerous other sites and blogs are jammed with personal postings, badly shot videos, and "jokey" photographs. Much of this material is amateurish and self-indulgent, and it attempts to focus the audience on a single individual ego acting out.

User-generated content, if thoughtfully and professionally executed, can tap into the universal language of a good story. Paul Theroux, the author, gave me valuable advice when he said, "Try and tell a personal story that branches out to a universal collective. Do not try it in reverse." Many students make this mistake. They ponder large world issues and miss the point that a story about their grandmother, if told correctly, can address world issues.

A personal example is my mother, the daughter of Swedish immigrants, who was brought up in a strict Pentecostal household where using profane language was forbidden. When she read the first story I wrote, she asked me to take out *the word*, the one she never had said or would ever say, immediately. We discussed freedom of speech (the universal issue).

The following week, while cooking breakfast for my father and me, she slammed a container of milk on the table, screaming "Marshall, here is your f*cking milk! If you are going to write like that then I am going to f*cking talk like that!"

Needless to say, I took the word out of my story.

David Smith, America's preeminent sculptor, was a guest speaker when I was a student at Pratt in 1960. He refused to evaluate or critique our artwork. He said, "Whether you prefer one of my artworks over another is of no interest to me. If I prefer one of your artworks over another should be of no interest to you. What should interest all of us are the stories we have to tell—what we have heard, seen, or experienced." Class time was spent telling stories. The storytelling migrated out of the classroom and continued well into the night at David Smith's favorite bar near the Brooklyn Navy Yard. If the purpose of teaching is to teach students how to learn, then that encounter has lasted a lifetime.

Now, in my late sixties, I have put together a book with over fifty stories that accompany my pictures. They are not a critical analysis of the illustrations, paintings, and sculpture I have done, but rather stories that surround the artwork. I will, of course, try and find a publisher, knowing that my chances of getting such a book published are slim. If I get no response, I will self-publish the book and put it up on my Web site. My options are open, inexpensive, and available, as they are for everybody.

The Adtritus of Viral and Guerrilla Advertising

Storytelling is central to branding, and branding is central to getting the word out about ideas, products, and things. Illustrators have been employed in the newest of new advertising methods that some call guerrilla and others call viral.

Viral, suggesting antibiotic-resistant disease, and *guerrilla*, implying terrorist warfare, became positive buzzwords during the late '90s, when American advertising appropriated them as labels for attitudinally edgy urban campaigns, also known as "never been done before" (NBDB) ads. This method (originally co-opted from alternative culture D-I-Y and wild postings) involves the semi-subversive planting of messages in venues and on objects ordinarily free of advertising, like banana peels, body tattoos, and urinal disinfectant pucks (presumably, it is difficult to forget a brand name after you've peed on it for a while). Viral and guerrilla strategies also depend on the unconventional employ of sidewalks, taxi roofs, and vacant storefronts to engender shock and awe, or at least surprise, in unsuspecting consumers. Illustrators are often hired to do them.

Illustrators have been involved in many of these ads, although not always as illustrators. Just because you draw doesn't mean you are locked into that role. Sometimes the illustrator is a good idea person; other times, the illustrator shines best as the designer or art director. In the world of NBDB ads, all kinds of talents are employed, often to do work they've never done before.

A few years ago, artists at Kirshenbaum Bond + Partners, in a burst of guerrilla-inspired pique, spray-painted some New York sidewalks with the line, "From here, it looks like you could use some new underwear," for an intimate clothing company. Last Christmas, an equally audacious "Good Samaritan" holiday campaign for Starbucks, created by Creature in Seattle, Washington, involved affixing red paper cups to roofs of dozens of cabs. If a "Samaritan" warned the taxi's passenger about the errant cup before the cab drove off, a free Starbucks gift card was given as a reward. During a Major League Baseball season, Ogilvy mounted a guerrilla action promoting the New York Mets where thin plastic sheets made to look like cracked windshields (as if a baseball had crashed through the glass) were placed on cars, accompanied by apology notes from Mets management. It was doubtless a heart-stopping surprise for victims who hopefully got a good laugh after realizing the joke.

These unorthodox ploys, also known as "ambient" advertising, have so successfully triggered buzz that some ad agencies and marketing companies obsessively comb metropolitan areas in order to commandeer public spaces—legally and otherwise. As a result new advertising detritus—or *adtritus*—is visible wherever the eye can see that has earned fervent proponents and angry detractors. Predictably, most advertising experts hold that the ersatz-grassroots approach is simply a new and viable means to put the word out—just another tool in their advertising media belt. But critics counter that it is just another desperate scramble to compete in an already over-saturated consumer marketplace, and litter both physical and mental environments in the bargain.

Whatever one's views, viral and guerrilla methods have been adopted for a very practical reason. "Advertising, for all its immensity and importance, is in trouble," writes NYU historian Stephen Duncombe in his new book *Dream: Re-Imaging Progressive Politics in an Age of Fantasy* (The New Press, 2007). With the advent of such anti-ad filters as TiVo, which allows TV viewers to eliminate advertising altogether, coupled with the downsizing of traditional advertising media—TV networks, newspapers and magazines—owing to competition from cable TV and the Internet, mainstream advertisers are finding it difficult to efficiently target audiences. Duncombe notes that ad spending started declining in 2001 for the first time in four decades, and by the largest percentage since the Depression. "Traditional spaces for advertising are drying up and consumers are harder to reach," he says. So if advertisers cannot identify new platforms from which to inveigle their way into hearts and minds, they will perish.

Of course, exploiting new media is not new. As far back as the '30s, for instance, advertisers conquered the heavens through skywriting and blimps. Whenever advanced technology is introduced, advertisers are among the first to adopt it. The colonization of virgin public space in many large cities is the latest frontier, and digital display technologies have made it infinitely easier to post, plaster, and affix scrims, vinyls, or decals in all sizes and shapes, and to project laser image messages on almost any surface. It appears that despite certain ordinances every nook, cranny, and scaffold is fair game. But how much "never been done before" advertising can or will the public tolerate before they feel their space has been violated like *never before?*

"No matter where it is, [NBDB advertising is] filled with equal amounts of shamelessness as well as ingenuity," insists Brian Collins, director of COLLINS: in New York. On the shameless side, he says there is a "plague of very suspicious 'restoration' scaffolding that covers ancient buildings entirely wrapped and smothered by ads for BMW and Mercedes Benz and Hollywood movies." On the clever side, he insists "this [guerrilla] thinking redefines what an 'ad' is." It's not enough to simply insinuate a brand into the public's subconscious through mainstream TV, print, or LED screens; inexpensive viral and guerrilla techniques are increasingly essential, either alone or as supplements to broader campaigns. Yet in order to not alienate the public, NBDB ads must provide something more tangible than a basic sales pitch.

The public will be annoyed by a guerrilla campaign that invades their space unless it "rewards them by giving some benefit," argues Rick Boyko, Managing Director of Virginia Commonwealth University's Adcenter. He says a superb example was Charmin's New York toilet pavilion during the 2006 holiday season. Rather than rent a typical Times Square bells-and-whistles billboard on Charmin's behalf, the Gigunda Group, experiential marketing consultants from Manchester, New Hampshire, took over an empty space and set up twenty well-designed, fully stocked, and meticulously maintained public restrooms. Since everyone appreciates clean public bathrooms, users were indebted to Charmin. But more important, Charmin garnered considerable press above and beyond the good will of a few hundred thousand people who, like me, used the facilities. Boyko, although he doesn't use the term NBDB, says it was NBDB at its best.

Most ambient, viral, guerrilla, or NBDB ads are not implicitly engaged in public service. I recently stumbled upon the stairway leading up from Pennsylvania Station to Seventh Avenue in New York City, which has become a prime place to post huge ads for commuter-targeted products. Just days before New Year's Eve 2007, the stairs were taken over by Kellogg's for the purpose of publicizing Special K Red Berries, and while it may seem that having pedestrians walk on a large bowl of strawberries and cereal flakes might adversely impact the brand's integrity by linking food to grimy shoes, the display's sheer spectacle of incongruous scale overcame most negative perceptions. And speaking of scale, sometimes gigantism is its own reward. Case in point: The hybrid billboard in Times Square last summer promoting Cingular cell phone company's claim of fewer dropped calls made a veritable splash (or crash), as it was precariously perched on the actual sidewalk to look as though it had literally "dropped" (get the metaphor?) from the scaffolding above (all that was missing was a pair of legs—like the Wicked Witch of the East—sticking out from underneath). Never mind that it actually blocked pedestrian space by causing a bottleneck and impeding foot traffic, the conceptual audacity and execution was enough to insure a positive experience. (It was also removed before it became too much of an annoyance.)

Guerrillas cannot afford to make enemies, but sometimes they do take calculated risks. For example, in 2006 MFK New York was commissioned to re-brand Rheingold, a legendary New York working-class beer that had gone out of business, to appeal to a hip, downtown clientele. Neil Powell, MFK's Chief Creative Officer, decided to use graffiti, which was still a controversial art form. "With a very limited budget, the decision was to get street traction," he explains. So when he scoped out the Lower East Side of Manhattan, and Brooklyn's Williamsburg, where the targeted consumers frequented bars and restaurants, he learned that local store-owners were responsible for keeping their "night shades," those protective pull-down gates, from being vandalized and actually paid fines when the shades were defaced. This triggered the idea to enlist local street artists to paint "whatever they wanted" on the gates, as long as somewhere they wrote in the word Rheingold—large or small. Ultimately, three blocks of Rivington Street were filled with the paintings. Both the artists, most of whom worked at night and were paid in cash or beer, and the store owners, who avoided fines and had newly painted shades, were happy. Even the community declared it a beautification program.

Not all, or even most, viral or guerrilla ads bring such satisfactory results. To truly succeed, the idea must be product-specific. Powell has refused to copy the Rheingold campaign for others because "it only works when it is appropriate." He has, however, found other NBDB venues: For Perry Ellis, MFK recently introduced graphic novels that tell an independent story while triggering a unique buzz for Perry, to dry-cleaning shirt boxes. In guerrilla campaigning, Brian Collins believes that "ads can go anywhere, as long as they add some delight, enhance, or improve the experience." But what happens when even this unconventional method becomes more and more predictable and commonplace? "Well," says Collins, "it's just more ugly, meaningless noise."

Chapter Three

Working in Traditional Media

To check the pulse of the illustration market, we went straight to those who spend their days and nights in the marketplace—the illustrators.

We sent out questionnaires to a wide range of artists—young and old, male and female, in the United States and abroad—who practice in the spectrum of media. We asked specifically what their last three jobs were and whether or not they were currently involved in meaningful or tangential ways with new platforms and technologies. Our goal was not to stack the decks for *or* against new or old, analog or digital, editorial or other, but rather to let the critical mass of illustrators tell us where the jobs were to be found. We also asked how new technology had impacted their respective practices, styles, and methodologies. We were surprised to learn that the majority of our respondents said they were primarily "traditional," insofar as they work for editorial and publishing clients.

Alex Murawski: Ad Man

What are the three most recent jobs you've done?

I have done several large images—one for use as a mural in a chain of Italian restaurants and the other for use as a movie festival poster—among other things.

Another project was a small piece for a spoken-word CD entitled Hairyman Meets Tailybone *for David Holt at High Windy Audio. The last was a poster image for The Blind Willie Blues Festival, [which is] held in Thomson, Georgia every spring. I guess that's four.*

Which of these jobs were done for a venue or medium that was untraditional (not editorial)?

For some reason, I started out doing a predominance of advertising imagery and only later got into editorial work. Perhaps because advertising imagery tends to employ a straight forward visual solution while editorial requires the ability to process and distill more complex issues into an effective visual gestalt, and it took me a while to get smart enough to do that. But advertising imagery remains at the core of my business.

How much of your work is done for traditional (i.e., print) and untraditional (i.e., digital, toys, textiles, murals) media?

Most of what I do is still for print of some kind or another, but recent projects have included expanded use in larger digital formats like murals, trade-show backdrops, and banners.

What is the most challenging untraditional medium you've worked in?

Since my work is a mix of traditional media (usually graphite or black ink washes) combined with digital color in Photoshop, I feel pretty comfortable dealing with the digital environment. But production technology and application always change with the times. The issue for me is the same as it was thirty years ago: getting the image right. For example, the mural I did for Marco's Pizza was difficult because of the intricacy of the initial pencil rendering. It was drawn in five separate pieces, then combined and colored in Photoshop. But scale for the final reproduction gave me pause. It was drawn about two feet wide and reproduced four times larger. Enlargement can be a sticky issue. It is said that reduction is your friend because it minimizes your mistakes. Conversely, with every mark amplified and enlarged, I find myself consumed with detail.

Who are your primary clients?

At this point in my career, I work with a small group of repeat clients in my area with an occasional incursion from the outside world. Think global, work local, I say. My wife likes to say I've segued from professional to dilettante.

What new technologies have you had to master?

Photoshop and the Web. Not much else for me so far. I do, however, rely on people with a high level of technological skills. So technical mastery is necessary by someone [in order] for me to do my work.

How has your illustration changed to meet the new technologies?

My drawing skills have come to the fore. My old work used to involve stipple rendering, film transparencies, and cel vinyl paint back painted on acetate. And that was after I did all the developmental drawing. Now I just draw in black and white, scan, manipulate, color, and send the work digitally. I find the easily editable digital environment fosters intuitive solutions that were unachievable for me in the past.

Alex Murawski illustration.

André Carrilho: Distorted Faces

What are the three most recent jobs you've done?

Recently, I've done an illustration for Word *magazine (London), another for* Diário de Notícias *(Lisbon), and I'm working on a children's book about Sandy Koufax for Schwartz & Wade Publications (NYC).*

Which of these jobs were done for a venue or medium that was untraditional (not editorial)?

All of these jobs were made for traditional media. I also work for untraditional media, but it's more difficult to get a financial comeback from these.

How much of your work is done for traditional (i.e., print) and untraditional (i.e., digital, toys, textiles, murals) media?

My main activity is as an illustrator for printed media (newspapers, magazines and books), but I'm trying to apply my drawing and design skills to other media.

I'm one of the two people who created a project called Video Jack. Video Jack ... develops work that ranges from VJing to audio-visual performances and multimedia interactive projects.

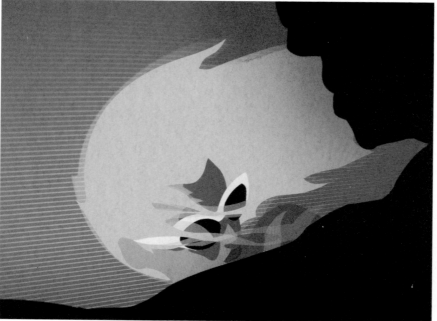

André Carrilho illustration.

What is the most challenging untraditional medium you've worked in?

More recently I was hired to decorate an entire floor of a hotel with illustrations. I haven't started the work yet, but I think it will be the most challenging to date.

Who are your primary clients?

Newspapers and magazines: The Independent on Sunday, Diário de Notícias, NZZ am Sonntag, Vanity Fair, Word *magazine.*

What new technologies have you had to master?

Adobe Flash, Illustrator (because Freehand is no longer produced), InDesign (because I don't use Quark anymore), iMovie (for basic animation editing).

How has your illustration changed to meet the new technologies?

Well, textures and effects that I usually use in Photoshop are not practical with vectorial animation. I had to adapt my style to a more clean look—something that can be easily animated by myself and others.

Anita Kunz: Self-Generated

What are the three most recent jobs you've done?

Well, the last three artworks I've done are as follows:
1. An ad for Barnes & Noble
2. A sketchbook illustration for Vanity Fair
3. A personal piece for a series I'm working on (uncommissioned)

Which of these jobs were done for a venue or media that was untraditional (not editorial)?

I'd say the ad was the most traditional in that the client had a definite idea about what she wanted. But I did use Photoshop in the post-production. I had to paint the New York [City] skyline and then make it appear to be moving quickly. I painted it traditionally and then manipulated it in Photoshop.

The illustration for Vanity Fair was traditional but it was an idea that I proposed, and that's fairly rare in the editorial world. It was a piece of stand-alone art, and didn't accompany any specific text. I wanted to do something about immigration and pitched the idea to the art director.

And the personal piece would most likely fall into the fine art category, although I'd like to find a print venue for it some day, either as part of a book or calendar. Despite the fact that I'm doing much more fine art, I still think like an illustrator and still love the idea of finding a larger audience for my work. And many subjects I'd love to address are being ignored by the mainstream media these days.

How much of your work is done for traditional (i.e., print) and untraditional (i.e., digital, toys, textiles, murals) media?

I guess I'm still largely traditional, although much of my work is self-generated these days. I'm coming up with ideas and trying to find a home for my ideas rather than waiting for the phone to ring and then reacting to text.

What is the most challenging untraditional medium you've worked in?

Well, I'm making pictures for myself, and I'm a very tough critic of my own work, so it's not easy!

Who are your primary clients?

Most of my paying clients are still magazines. I do a bit of advertising and book work as well.

Anita Kunz illustration.

What new technologies have you had to master?

I haven't really felt the need to master anything other than systems that would help me communicate more easily with clients. I don't feel compelled to make art digitally, although I find the Internet wonderful for research.

And clients want easier access to sketches these days, and also to finalized art, so I now am able to scan my pictures, tweak in Photoshop if necessary, and send via e-mail or upload to FTP sites. I wouldn't say I've mastered anything, though!

How has your illustration changed to meet the new technologies?

Well, my best work I think is still untouched by the new technologies. My biggest challenges are as always to try and come up with good ideas and attempt to capture aspects of the zeitgeist. I see the new technologies as wonderful tools, but I try not to use them as a crutch.

Brett Ryder: Making 2-D into 3-D

What are the three most recent jobs you've done?

At the moment, I'm working on the Guardian Glastonbury project, which is for their tent and their festival identity. I'm working on an art issue cover for a magazine called Ritz Carlton *in America, and a book jacket for* Think *by Edward De Bono.*

Which of these jobs were done for a venue or medium that was untraditional (not editorial)?

The Guardian commission is one of those fun jobs where you can let your imagination go wild. [I'm creating] images to go on their festival vans and to decorate their tent, and also maps and bags for the festival-goers.

How much of your work is done for traditional (i.e., print) and untraditional (i.e., digital, toys, textiles, murals) media?

99 percent is for print; the other work is rare for me but a pleasure to do.

What is the most challenging untraditional medium you've worked in?

Working on a short 3-D animation with a friend. It taught me a lot about how to approach my 2-D illustration. Producing an animation can be an epic task—[in this case,] one we never completed—but a very rewarding venture, if slightly disappointing, as neither of us like to leave unfinished projects.

Who are your primary clients?

Editorial clients, [which are] some of the best to work for.

What new technologies have you had to master?

I wouldn't say I was a technophobe, but I have little interest in new technology until I need to, if you get my drift. I have just bought a new iMac with a new operating system and Photoshop, etc. I had owned my old computer for about six years, so you can imagine the learning curve, but I certainly wouldn't say I'd mastered it.

How has your illustration changed to meet the new technologies?

I think your work naturally changes when you use new technology. It opens new doors and makes old tasks easier, as long as you embrace it and try to have fun, which is an art in itself.

Brett Ryder illustration.

42

Brian Cronin: Suiting Himself

What are the three most recent jobs you've done?

1. *Five book jacket covers for Penguin UK for a series of science fiction classic books by John Wyndham:* The Day of the Triffids, The Chrysalids, The Midwich Cuckoos, The Kracken Wakes, *and* The Trouble with Lichen
2. *An op-ed for the* New York Times *about writers who lie*
3. *An illustration for Wellesley College for an article about the continuation of learning after graduation*

How much of your work is done for traditional (i.e., print) and untraditional (i.e., digital, toys, textiles, murals) media?

Almost all!

What is the most challenging untraditional medium you've worked in?

I did a series of stamps for The Irish Post Office (fig an Poist), and a mural for the Transportation Museum gift shop in Grand Central Station (New York).

Who are your primary clients?

Outside *magazine,* Entertainment Weekly, *Wellesley College,* Reader's Digest, *and Penguin books.*

What new technologies have you had to master?

Photoshop.

How has your illustration changed to meet the new technologies?

My work changes to suit myself and the decade in which I'm living, but I don't think technology has had any impact, really, on my work.

Brian Cronin illustration.

Charles Wilkin: Designer / Illustrator

What are the three most recent jobs you've done?
A cover for Deliver *magazine (US Postal Service), an opener for* Chicago *magazine, and a cover and opener for* Seattle Metropolitan *magazine.*

How much of your work is done for traditional (i.e., print) and untraditional (i.e., digital, toys, textiles, murals) media?
I would say 90 percent of my work is done for traditional print media: mostly magazines and advertising.

What is the most challenging untraditional medium you've worked in?
I did a mural for PS 186 in the Bronx. I had never done a mural before or a piece on that kind of scale. The challenge wasn't so much the technical end of it, but more of creating something that had lived in an environment. The mural had to work in conjunction with the architecture while at the same time being able to stand alone. It was very difficult, for sure.

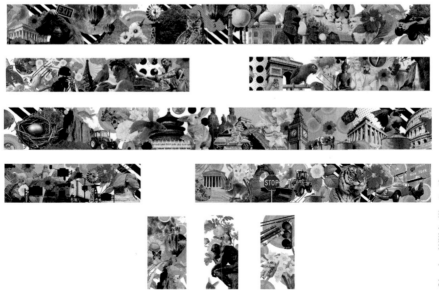

Charles Wilkin illustrations.

Who are your primary clients?

I have a variety of clients in the music, art, and fashion industries, as well as magazines, ad agencies, and large corporations. I have, in the past, worked for Target, Epson, Adobe, Burton Snowboards, Nixon Watches, and Mattel.

What new technologies have you had to master?

Really just Photoshop—not really a new technology, but I have had to expand my skills. My work is getting more and more complex and requires a lot more Photoshop work than it used to.

How has your illustration changed to meet the new technologies?

Yes, some. I used to work half by hand, half digital. Now I work almost 95 percent digital. Which is fine because, ultimately, it's faster. Plus my work has evolved into something a bit cleaner and even more layered, so going digital seemed like a natural step forward.

Craig Frazier: Disciplined

What are the three most recent jobs you've done?

A Wall Street Journal *full-page editorial, a United States Postal Service stamp, and wine packaging.*

Which of these jobs were done for a venue or medium that was untraditional (not editorial)?

I did limited-edition wine labels: a suite of three labels for a Realm Cellars Wine called Absurd. I was responsible for the illustration and design of these labels.

How much of your work is done for traditional (i.e., print) and untraditional (i.e., digital, toys, textiles, murals) media?

95 percent of my work is traditional. The only product work is book design and illustration.

What is the most challenging untraditional medium you've worked in?

I find postage stamps particularly difficult because of the the subjects assigned and the approval process. The public permanence of them tends to scare the spontaneity right out of the process for me. They take a lot of discipline to arrive at something good.

Who are your primary clients?

Publications like BusinessWeek, *the* Harvard Business Review, *the* Wall Street Journal, New York Times *op-eds, and* Time, *[as well as] corporate clients like MasterCard, Navigant Consulting, Boeing, and United Airlines.*

What new technologies have you had to master?

Nothing new since Photoshop and Illustrator.

Wine labels designed by Craig Frazier.

How has your illustration changed to meet the new technologies?

Not much.

Dan Page: Plywood and Digital

What are the three most recent jobs you've done?

I've recently worked on an editorial job for Golf Digest Index, *which is a book of short stories related to golf, published by* Golf Digest *magazine. I produced two images for a story called 'Down The Stretch,' which illustrated how yoga [is] good for your golf game. Another job was a full page for* Money *magazine, and the subject matter was how to use your home to leverage your child's education costs. My third most recent assignment was for* Time *magazine. It was a review for a book called* Nudge.

How much of your work is done for traditional (i.e., print) and untraditional (i.e., digital, toys, textiles, murals) media?

99 percent of my work is done for traditional print media. Out of that I'd say 85 percent is done for the editorial magazine market. I'm drawn to that work. It allows the creative freedom that I desire.

Illustration by Dan Page.

What is the most challenging untraditional medium you've worked in?

I recently did work for a gallery show where I had to design an image that was printed on an actual pillow. I had to consider the three-dimensional quality of the pillow when developing my image, so it was a deviation from my usual two-dimensional work. Not very challenging, but different.

Who are your primary clients?

I mainly work with editorial clients, but I also do projects for book publishers, design firms, and advertising agencies.

What new technologies have you had to master?

Even though I work traditionally on plywood with acrylic and ink, the computer is becoming an integral part of the process. In the last five years, I've enhanced my traditional approach with the digital medium more and more each year. Sometimes I fear there's too much of an influence on my work so I pull back, then I dive in again. I put my images together in Photoshop. Every week I seem to learn something new and use the new trick within my work.

How has your illustration changed to meet the new technologies?

It's changed in positive ways. I find that the computer allows me to experiment with color and technique in quick, easy steps. Through these experimentations my work evolves. I am able to produce more work, in a shorter period of time. A few years ago, I [had] to photograph my finals at a photographer's studio, then out source the film developing, and then courier the 4×5 transparency. This was very time-consuming and would take a whole afternoon.

Douglas Fraser: Hannibal Vector

What are the three most recent jobs you've done?

I've done an illustration for the Ford motor company, a half-page illustration for Fortune Small Business *magazine, and a half-page for* Forbes *magazine.*

Which of these jobs were done for a venue or medium that was untraditional (not editorial)?

The Ford assignment was for the Internet and other possible promotional products, not traditional print.

How much of your work is done for traditional (i.e., print) and untraditional (i.e., digital, toys, textiles, murals) media?

The majority of my assignments are still print-based. I would say about 85 percent of my assignments are still print (traditional).

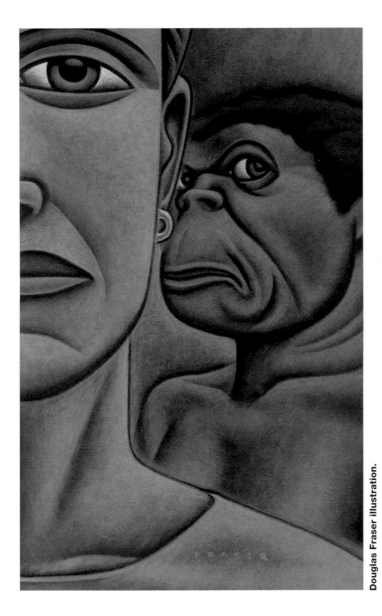

Douglas Fraser illustration.

What is the most challenging untraditional medium you've worked in?

The most challenging untraditional medium for me has not always been so. For me it would be mural assignments. Murals are a medium that has suffered a growing strangulation with the increase in technology. The committee aspect was held at bay when I developed the illustration with traditional media, pencil, and paint and brush. Now with the aid of the computer, the aspirations of the committee reach more deeply into the construction of the design, and final execution. A large-scale digital mural (venue site) is the most challenging for me these days.

Who are your primary clients?

My primary clients are advertisers, with editorial assignments coming in second. I would say that [they are] about 65 percent advertising (and institutional), and 35 percent editorial.

What new technologies have you had to master?

The basic computer skills, some Photoshop, Adobe Illustrator, and uploading FTP material. The Web site updating and maintenance is time-consuming. Also, scanning and creating final art files in place of the shooting of transparencies has downloaded more production aspects onto the on going list of my responsibilities.

How has your illustration changed to meet the new technologies?

I've been able to explore more possibilities in my choice of expression and execution. I initially went to the computer in an evolutionary manner. Over time, it has made my traditional brush and paint in my studio sometimes feel out of place. Although I have found that a union of my love of the traditionally painted surface, married with the color and construction on the computer, has helped meet the more pressing deadlines of today. Also, I've worked in vector programs for applications that have strict printing demands. Working with a vector program came out of the graphic ideas I wanted to explore but found frustrating with a brush at the time.

Ed Lam: Wading in Bogs

What are the three most recent jobs you've done?

1. A book jacket illustration for a young adult novel, The Story of Jonas *by Maurine Dahlberg*

2. *Illustration and design of a laminated foldout,* A Guide to Northeastern Dragonflies and Damselflies, *for the Massachusetts Audubon Society*

3. *Writing and illustrations for the* Peterson Field Guide to North American Dragonflies *(in progress)*

How much of your work is done for traditional (i.e., print) and untraditional (i.e., digital, toys, textiles, murals) media?

Almost everything I've done in recent memory has been for print. The one exception was a series of insects I did for the Newark Museum. They were having an exhibit on social insects, i.e., bees, ants, and termites, and wanted large illustrations of the different castes to go on the wall. Because of the time constraints, I did the job completely digitally, something I had done only once previously.

What is the most challenging untraditional medium you've worked in?

What I do in preparation for the work in the field guide, like wading in bogs and swamps and collecting specimens, is not typical for an illustrator.

Who are your primary clients?

Currently Houghton Mifflin, since I'm living off the advance of the dragonfly guide. Previously, it was the New York Times.

What new technologies have you had to master?

In recent years, I learned to use a stylus and pad. I had been doing all my preliminary work on the computer, sketches and layout, then transferring the

Insect illustration by Ed Lam.

sketch onto a piece of paper to paint on. Now the illustrations for the dragonfly guide will be done digitally in Photoshop, layouts in InDesign rather than Quark. I'm a traditionalist at heart and it pains me not to have a painting on paper to look at at the end of the day, but with over two thousand illustrations planned for the job, I need to save time and maintain accuracy, so I'll get over it. I don't have to physically mix colors or wash my brushes. And every client wants the piece delivered digitally these days so you might as well skip the scanner. I remember handing a piece to Steve at the [New York Times] Book Review and he told me I was the only illustrator who still dropped off his work, so I was a bit behind the curve. I started e-mailing scans, but then I never did get to see Steve anymore.

How has your illustration changed to meet the new technologies?

I hope it hasn't. My methodology has changed, but I'm trying to keep people from knowing whether a work is digital or not. As I did that early digital job for the Newark Museum, I had to be satisfied that it looked like my painting since that's what the client and I expected. Luckily, the way I apply paint in acrylics seems to translate well into Photoshop. I only did one Book Review *cover completely digitally: that roster of chefs dubbed 'The Hunger Artists.' Could you tell?*

Graham Roumieu: Placemats?

What are the three most recent jobs you've done?

A cover and a series of thirty interior images for a book of curious factoids about wine, an image for a weekly newspaper column I contribute to, and a series of spots for a national news magazine.

Which of these jobs were done for a venue or medium that was untraditional (not editorial)?

Not including the likelihood that the editorial images will probably show up on the Web as a part of extended rights, none of the images was for untraditional media. It is possible that the images for the book could one day appear on products like placemats, T-shirts, and keychains. They probably won't, but that possibility was taken into consideration when the contract for the work was negotiated. All the cool kids are going to want those placemats.

How much of your work is done for traditional (i.e., print) and untraditional (i.e., digital, toys, textiles, murals) media?

The large majority of my work is still done for traditional clients, but, like I mentioned, with my work, traditional clients often exercise their extended rights to images for things like online editions. Of the many jobs I've done in the relatively short time I have been working, very few of them have been usages that weren't primarily print-based for editorial and book publishing. Projects conceived purely for untraditional as a percentage of my overall volume would be in the single digits. Nonetheless, tons of my images appear online because of the Web archives of publications. Books that I write and illustrate owe a lot of their success to publicity they get online, including sometimes pages being scanned and posted on blogs. Though I've never received photo evidence, several people have threatened to tattoo my work on their bodies. Indie bands will 'borrow' low-res images off of my Web site and produce photocopied gig posters around my artwork that I will then see stapled to a telephone pole in my neighborhood, thus closing the new vs. old medium circle of life. To beat the point to death, it has been my experience that even the most traditionally-intended work is very likely to bleed into untraditional media.

What is the most challenging untraditional medium you've worked in?

I worked with an ad agency on a rather cool and novel Web site for a beer company in Canada. The concept was that it was an old-fashioned beer company that logically had an old-fashioned Web site. Instead of just loading like a standard site, the content was hand-rendered by a grumpy, Web site-rendering artist. I played the grumpy Web site renderer from the mid-forearm down. It required a couple of full days of me sitting in a film production studio being shot from overhead by a digital camera, drawing out the numerous pieces of content for the site, but also playing the role of a performer, which takes the already difficult job of drawing on spec and adds the difficulty of drawing on cue.

Aside from that, I've worked on short films based on my work with an animation studio in which, even though I wasn't playing the part of an animator and was just supplying background and basic character art, still worked out to be (not surprisingly) an incredible amount of work; work that forced me to make considerations about motion and timing that I otherwise wouldn't have to with my day-to-day image-making.

There was also the assignment where I followed a travel writer friend of mine on the five-day drive from New York to Los Angeles portion of his around-the-world trip. At the end of every day, he would blog about his trip and I would supply an image to go with his post. Almost no different from any other editorial job, except with most editorial jobs you don't have to drive thirteen hours a day, then take five minutes in a hotel room to distill your thirteen hours of experience and thousands of kilometers of scenes down into one drawing that has to be OK'd by an editor and be posted by the next morning.

Who are your primary clients?

I do most of my work for editorial clients in Canada, the United States, and the UK.

What new technologies have you had to master?

Syncing my iCalendar to my wall calendar.

How has your illustration changed to meet the new technologies?

Not in any exceptional way. For Web, resolution is a bit of an issue so I'll usually make an image simpler, especially if it is going to run smaller. [They're] hardly any different from the same sorts of considerations a good illustrator would make for print, though. For things like products and merchandise, it's mostly about decoration, so I can still be smart and funny with the images. I guess I don't really feel like I have to nail some concept that is going to stop the viewer from flipping to the next page like I do with editorial work. It's still about making arresting images, though, just with slightly different applications.

Graham Roumieu illustration.

Guy Billout: More Hybrids

What are the three most recent jobs you've done?

1. Bicycling *magazine: a full page for a story about the ten toughest stretches of road in the US*

Guy Billout illustration for *Travel & Leisure* magazine, drawn in black-and-white with a technical pen, then scanned and colored in Photoshop.

2. Travel & Leisure *magazine: a half page for a story about strategies to travel in Europe with a weak dollar*

3. Mother Jones *magazine: one-third of a page for a story about burning fossil fuels versus new ecological technologies*

How much of your work is done for traditional (i.e., print) and untraditional (i.e., digital, toys, textiles, murals) media?

If illustrations done exclusively for use on a Web site are considered untraditional, *this would be the only untraditional work I have done so far. Under that definition, untraditional constitutes less than 10 percent of my work. Typically, the images created for this type of assignment are made with a traditional black-and-white drawing, scanned on Photoshop in order to be colored digitally.*

What is the most challenging untraditional medium you've worked in?

Learning to use Photoshop (if Photoshop is considered a medium).

Who are your primary clients?

Magazines and corporations.

What new technologies have you had to master?

Photoshop and e-mail (phone and fax appear to be more and more irrelevant).

How has your illustration changed to meet the new technologies?

Formally, it has not changed my illustration very much, except for the originals. [It] always started with a black-and-white line drawing, and was sometimes partly colored with the airbrush. These originals completed on Photoshop end up somehow as hybrids that cannot be offered or sold as whole originals.

Hadley Hooper: Print Is Where the Heart Is

What are the three most recent jobs you've done?

1. New York Times Book Review *cover*

2. *Bi-monthly column for Michelle Slatalla's 'Cyberfamilias' for the* New York Times

3. *Drawings for Web animation for Solis Hotels Web page*

Which of these jobs were done for a venue or medium that was untraditional (not editorial)?

The drawings for Solis Hotels are going to be used on the Web only. The other images were used in print but also have a small Web presence on the New York Times *Web site.*

How much of your work is done for traditional (i.e., print) and untraditional (i.e., digital, toys, textiles, murals) media?

Most of the work is still for print media.

What is the most challenging untraditional medium you've worked in?

Animation for Web.

Who are your primary clients?

Primarily I am an editorial illustrator; that's where my heart is. Typically I'll do one or two large advertising jobs in a year; that's where the money is.

Last year I did eleven new label designs for Dekuyper Liqueurs. The Solis Hotels job, which is lapping into 2008, includes in-room collateral and Web-only applications, so [it consists of] print and Web.

What new technologies have you had to master?

I haven't mastered Photoshop, but have been using it since the mid '90s and sort of know what I need to know. I bet I use 20 percent of its potential.

I'm experimenting with a new print-making technique called 'polyester plate lithography.' I want to continue to use techniques that use traditional materials like paint and ink to keep the work looking like there is a hand involved.

Digital technologies can be very seductive; I scan all my work and send it as digital files. Once they are scanned in, I inevitably change the color, size, or some aspect, thus creating an image that has no physical artifact.

How has your illustration changed to meet the new technologies?

I have moved from oils to 'dry' media like house paint, acrylics, and inks—things that dry quickly and can be placed face-down on a scanner or popped into an envelope.

When I was beginning to work as an illustrator, I was still using oil paints and quick-dryers so that I could FedEx the finals. This was the mid '90s when we weren't yet sending digital files. I got an assignment from David Carson for Raygun *magazine. He wanted a painting of a simple knife isolated on the page. I quickly got to work, and when it was time to put [the piece] into the envelope to send, it was still a bit wet. I found a piece of wax tissue from a cigar box, lightly covered the image, and sent it off.*

A month later, when the magazine was published, I was surprised and embarrassed to see that the image had been published with the tissue still attached. I wasn't sure whether I should tell David or pretend that I had meant to do that.

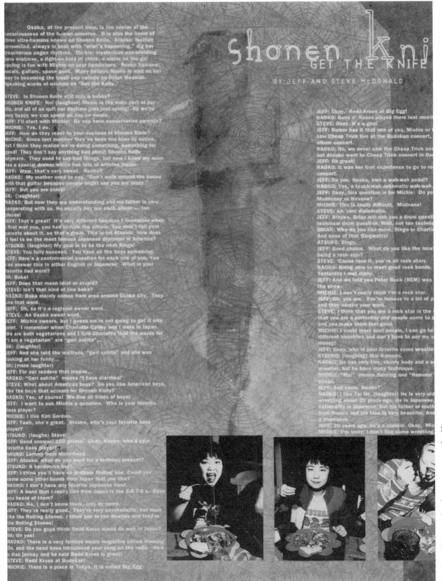

Hadley Hooper's tissue-paper knife.

I ended up telling him, and he was quite happy with the art with the paper stuck to it. It took about a year to transition to a new medium and it changed the look of my work from the softer look of oils to a much more graphic look.

Harriet Russell: More Texture

What are the three most recent jobs you've done?

1. *An identity for a children's publisher called Lampyro, commissioned by a design company in Mexico. The brief was very open and creative, and [the company] wanted several images for use on business cards, stationery, brochures, book bags, etc.*
2. *Illustrations for the Royal Society for the Prevention of Cruelty to Animals (RSPCA) annual review. Cover illustration, three inside, and some additional hand-rendered lettering.*
3. *Illustrations for Kid's Club, a special club for kids living in a very upmarket new housing development in LA. Cover for activities brochure, T-shirt design, birthday card, and hand-rendered lettering.*

Which of these jobs were done for a venue or medium that was untraditional (not editorial)?

Parts of both the Lampyro and Kid's Club jobs would perhaps count as untraditional, I think (book bags, T-shirts etc.).

How much of your work is done for traditional (i.e., print) and untraditional (i.e., digital, toys, textiles, murals) media?

So far, the large majority of my work has been commissioned for traditional media for various printed products—book covers, editorials, packaging, brochures, etc. On occasion, I have had work animated for use on the Web (for handbag company Radley, and for the Canadian Centre for Architecture [CCA]) but the work has been primarily commissioned for print.

What is the most challenging untraditional medium you've worked in?

Well, this was a while ago, but I once did some large drawings (murals) for the transport museum in Glasgow. This was quite challenging, as I rarely work that big. And once I did some chalk drawings on a big blackboard as part of an advert for Christian Aid Week. They didn't use them in the end, actually, but it was quite a challenge, as there wasn't much margin for error and I had to go to the set and draw them there [as opposed to sitting] at a desk like normal.

Who are your primary clients?

Publishers, including Random House, Hodder and Orion, and Italian publisher Edizioni Corraini. Design companies that commission illustrations for packaging, sometimes books. Newspapers and magazines: for example, the Guardian, Sainsbury's *magazine, and the* Independent on Sunday.

What new technologies have you had to master?

I'm using the computer a lot more than when I first started, as I quite often used to screen print work. I still do [the work by hand] sometimes, but often it's not an option as it can be very time consuming.

How has your illustration changed to meet the new technologies?

When I first started to use the computer, I think [my work] it went through a stage of looking quite flat; however, now I try to get more texture in to retain a hand-done feel.

Harriet Russell illustration.

61

Jashar Awan: Digitally Dependent

What are the three most recent jobs you've done?

I just turned in a spot for the New Yorker *about a documentary on Iraq's only heavy metal band. Last week I did an illustration and spot for a story to be*

1/30

Illustration by Jashar Awan.

featured in L *magazine about renting a room in a decaying Upper East Side penthouse. Those were preceded by another* New Yorker *illustration.*

How much of your work is done for traditional (i.e., print) and untraditional (i.e., digital, toys, textiles, murals) media?

Most of my work has been done for print. However, the work is often reused on the magazine's or newspaper's Web site. I have done some illustration for untraditional media (such as mock-up character designs for an online ad campaign) but print work puts the roof over my head.

What is the most challenging untraditional medium you've worked in?

It's not illustration work, but after having built my own Web site, I received requests to do portfolio sites for other illustrators. These Web sites led me to design work for Pink Elephant Projects (PEP) Gallery in Brooklyn, where I was eventually asked to curate an annual illustration show.

Who are your primary clients?

The New Yorker *and* American Medical News.

What new technologies have you had to master?

I'm always learning new ways of using Photoshop.

How has your illustration changed to meet the new technologies?

Photoshop has influenced my approach to illustration from the beginning. I'm able to digitally clean up sketches, color my drawings, and design illustrations. However, I have to be careful not to rely too much on the program or let it overpower my drawings, creating a look that is 'Photoshoppy.' Drawing will always be the most important skill in illustration, while new technologies should be seen as tools to make work faster and easier.

Joe Ciardiello: Shorter Deadlines

What are the three most recent jobs you've done?

1. A spot for the back essay page for Time *magazine*

2. *A piece for* Golf Digest *(a Condé Nast publication)*
3. *A portrait for the* New York Times Book Review

Joe Ciardiello illustration.

How much of your work is done for traditional (i.e., print) and untraditional (i.e., digital, toys, textiles, murals) media?

All my work is created traditionally, then scanned and e-mailed. I'd say the clients are 85 percent traditional (print) and 15 percent untraditional (digital or online).

What is the most challenging untraditional medium you've worked in?

The process is really no different for me.

Who are your primary clients?

Magazines, newspapers, and book publishers. The one steady untraditional client is www.barnesandnoble.com, where I do portraits for the B&N Review section.

What new technologies have you had to master?

I'd hardly say I've mastered anything. I don't embrace the technology easily. Scanning and adjusting images to e-mail is pretty much the extent of it for now.

How has your illustration changed to meet the new technologies?

[I'm] adapting to shorter deadlines, doing most of my research online, and working a bit smaller and on whiter paper (for scanning).

Josh Cochran: Got Milk?

What are the three most recent jobs you've done?

I did a portrait of the band battles for Beautiful/Decay *magazine, a black-and-white drawing for the* New York Times *op-ed page, and conceptual sketches for an online 'Got Milk?' campaign.*

Which of these jobs were done for a venue or medium that was untraditional (not editorial)?

The character and vehicle sketches for the 'Got Milk?' campaign are untraditional. The pitch did not get approved in the end, but the drawings were meant for an interactive 'Got Milk?' Web site.

How much of your work is done for traditional (i.e., print) and untraditional (i.e., digital, toys, textiles, murals) media?

Most of my work is done for print/editorial, and maybe a quarter of the work I do is for untraditional media such as murals, Web graphics, tote bags, etc.

What is the most challenging untraditional medium you've worked in?

A forty-foot-long mural produced digitally for the Liberty Science Center, a children's museum in New Jersey. I had a hard time meeting some of the requests of the client. They would ask for very specific characters holding scientific instruments, i.e., a young African-American girl between the ages of nine and twelve, holding a light prism. Another factor that made this medium particularly tough was figuring out how I could up-res my digital files to fill a forty-foot-long space.

Who are your primary clients?

Recently, I've been doing the most work for the New York Times *and Sterling Publishing.*

What new technologies have you had to master?

Photoshop and vectorizing in Illustrator are probably the big ones.

How has your illustration changed to meet the new technologies?

I have started to draw in layers. I think this started because I've worked with motion graphics companies that always need my work to be separated [into] background, figure, arms, etc. This has helped me realize a whole other spatial quality that is starting to emerge in my illustration.

Josh Cochran's Liberty Science Center mural.

Mark Ulrickson: Man of New Yorker

What are the three most recent jobs you've done?

1. *A* New Yorker *cover about the Eliot Spitzer imbroglio, entitled 'The Emperor's New Clothes'*
2. *A poster for Gundlach-Bundschu winery for a one-person play about the history of the winery*
3. *Concept sketches for murals at Soldier Field (football stadium) for United Airlines and the Chicago Bears*

Which of these jobs were done for a venue or medium that was untraditional (not editorial)?

The mural project certainly fits that bill. It was done for the BDM, a Minneapolis ad agency.

How much of your work is done for traditional (i.e., print) and untraditional (i.e., digital, toys, textiles, murals) media?

90 percent is done for traditional media. The untraditional includes the mural project for United Airlines/Chicago Bears, concept sketches for a line of dog purses, and some Web site drawings that were slightly animated for a site that is basically a fun questionnaire for graphic designers.

What is the most challenging untraditional medium you've worked in?

The football stadium murals could be, but we're still at the initial sketch stage. The animated drawings for the questionnaire were difficult in that I had to do one hundred-plus drawings that didn't always align correctly for the animators and I was new to the process.

Who are your primary clients?

Magazines are foremost, [along with] personal commissions for dog portraits and family portraits. The New Yorker *is by far my most consistent (and important) client.*

What new technologies have you had to master?

Not many, but I do use iPhoto a lot to archive my work and I am currently having to find and reload thousands of images. I had crashed my iPhoto library by loading a raw image and so set about collecting and reloading files onto my external drive. However, my ten-year-old daughter inadvertently knocked over my external drive, breaking it and losing all of my recovered scanned pieces. One technology I need to master is the backing-up of the backups.

How has your illustration changed to meet the new technologies?

Not much. I still send originals to clients, but will back up the work by scanning it first, provided there's time for that. Occasionally I'll e-mail the finish to a client. I do find that I use Google for research all of the time.

Illustration by Mark Ulrickson.

Matt Rotta: Killer Tomatoes

What are the three most recent jobs you've done?

I am finishing up a job now for 3×3 magazine. Charles Hively, the editor, is putting together a cheap-eats NYC restaurant guide. For every restaurant listed, I do a location drawing of that restaurant. There are thirteen black-and-white drawings for the whole book.

Before that, I worked on a piece for the New York Times *op-ed. The story was about the anniversary of the Tet Offensive.*

And before that I did a job for the Russian version of Esquire. *I don't know the topic, as they did not send the article, but they wanted a composition based on work they had seen on my Web site, and told me the content and concept they wanted. The description they asked for was a horizontal piece, with a line of famous robots (Terminator, C-3PO, Optimus Prime, etc.) waiting to get through a metal detector at the airport.*

How much of your work is done for traditional (i.e., print) and untraditional (i.e., digital, toys, textiles, murals) media?

So far, most of the work I get is in the arena of editorial, and occasionally, a comic job pops up as well. A couple of years ago I did a series of drawings for the design firm PW Feats. The drawings were for a Catholic Charities benefit. Originally, they were to be used on the program books. The drawings of hands using various tools ended up being enlarged and printed on six-foot-tall panels, and were arranged to make the stage set for the benefit.

What is the most challenging untraditional medium you've worked in?

Most of what I do is fairly traditional. I have designed an album cover that was for an exclusive online album. If the album is bought, the customer has the option to also download and print the cover, an apparent side effect of the iTunes generation. I am in the process of talking with the producer of a possible remake of Attack of the Killer Tomatoes. *He wants to commission some art from me to start an awareness campaign for a younger audience about the film. My art may end up online, on T-shirts, or on posters. The producer isn't sure of everything he wants to use the image for, so we are in the process of talking about legalities. Because the movie characters are copyrighted, that complicates things.*

Who are your primary clients?

Mostly the New York Times, *as well as the* Utne Reader. *Others have been* LA Weekly, Esquire Russia, *and an assortment of other magazines. All my primary work comes from editorial.*

What new technologies have you had to master?

Photoshop is an absolutely essential technology to master. Dreamweaver has been really good to know; it gives me freedom to play with my Web site. Technology seems to be most useful with things like promotion. InDesign is good for laying out my work in book form and for designing cards. A lot of [the work] is finding resources online, and knowing how to use them. If you know InDesign, you can lay out a book, go to [the Web site] Lulu.com, and have your own beautiful-looking book printed. Makes doing it yourself much easier.

Matt Rotta illustration.

How has your illustration changed to meet the new technologies?

My work is traditional in the sense that it relies mostly on basic drawing skills. Illustration is reprinted through a digital intermediary, and the digital process alters your original color, so knowing how to control color digitally in my work became essential. I stopped trying to use color outside of the computer, and started coloring all my original work monochromatically and finishing it on the computer. Then I started doing art in pieces, and assembling it on the computer. I would do a line drawing in three different pieces, scan them, and arrange them in Photoshop, then do painted color on another sheet of paper or several. Altogether, I would have six different pieces of paper, all being assembled into one work. Once the piece was done and printed, it would be hard to tell that it was a digital illustration. The point of going through such a process for something that in the end does not look digital at all is to have control over all of the different parts, and to make changes that might be needed later very easily. It also enforces the idea that the final in illustration is the printed piece, not the sum of parts.

Michael Schwab: Unchanged

What are the three most recent jobs you've done?

1. *City of New Orleans (print advertising, banners, etc.), Amtrak/Arnold Worldwide*
2. *'Bison Logo' (non-profit organization logo), Denver Mountain Parks*
3. *'Recycle or Die' (serigraph print and metal sculpture), The Chase Group*

What of these jobs were done for a venue or media is untraditional (not editorial)?

I would consider the re-introduction of my 1991 poster, 'Recycle or Die' (originally created for an American Institute of Graphic Arts [AIGA] exhibit), as untraditional because this image, among other archival work, is being re-worked for very large-format, fine art serigraph prints, as well as metal sculptures for the fine art market.

How much of your work is done for traditional (i.e., print) and untraditional (i.e., digital, toys, textiles, murals) media?

Most of my work is created for print at this time. Currently in production are a select collection of large serigraph prints and metal sculpture projects for a fine art publisher. I also designed a Pendleton blanket for Wells Fargo Bank a year or two ago.

What is the most challenging untraditional medium you've worked in?

Packaging is difficult: [there are] too many rules and brand strategy concepts.

Michael Schwab's Pendleton blanket design for Wells Fargo.

Who are your primary clients?

Arnold Worldwide (AMTRAK), Wells Fargo, The Golden Gate National Parks Conservancy, various wine-country clients, and small local clients.

What new technologies have you had to master?

Digital color. Until recently, it has been difficult to technically calibrate color specifications for monitors and printers and to then maintain those colors (Pantone, CMYK, coated stock, uncoated stock, newspaper, Web). It takes time.

How has your illustration changed to meet the new technologies?

My style of illustration (my approach to image, type, layout, concept, positive/ negative space, color, etc.) has remained unchanged through the years. I begin projects the way I always have: initial pencil sketches on vellum, then pen and ink (Rapidograph) on paper. However—and this is where my technique has changed—the original inking is then scanned and brought to the computer screen for fine-tuning line work, making color decisions, and creating digital files [that are] ready to print. Digital production is so much cleaner and more organized than it was in the old days. It works. However, I became a graphic artist because of my love of the craft. I have always enjoyed working with traditional tools—T-square, compass, French curve, pencil, pen, ink, X-Acto knife, proportion scale, etc. So far, there is no computer on my drawing table.

Monika Aichele: Inflatable Monkeys

What are the three most recent jobs you've done?

1. *A CD cover for the audio-book of* The World Is Round *by Gertrude Stein*
2. *An illustration for a pharmaceutical company's in-house magazine about doing business in Scandinavia*
3. *An illustration for a medical column in the* SZ-Magazin *(Wissen) on constructional apraxia*

How much of your work is done for traditional (i.e., print) and untraditional (i.e., digital, toys, textiles, murals) media?

95 percent is still traditional.

What is the most challenging untraditional medium you've worked in?

For Stefan Sagmeister, I designed three-dimensional, ten-meter-high, inflatable monkey sculpures. Going from two-dimensional work to three-dimensional work was a very intense change. I had to think of an illustration you could walk around. Each angle and perspective should offer an interesting view. Due to the size, [when] standing in front of the sculpture, you would only see parts of it; you would not be at the same height and you would not have the chance to look at it eye to eye. [The monkeys] were supposed to look angry, so I tried to keep the facial expression simple.

I also had to consider the stability of these gigantic animals and the effect of the wind, which influenced the posture of the sculptures. Now that I've seen the monkey sculptures in different environments, I am always surprised how different they look. Their expressions change quite a bit with different surroundings. It's almost as if [they are] living illustrations, moving when the wind blows, struggling with the strings holding them to the ground.

Enormous inflatable monkey created by Monika Aichele.

Who are your primary clients?

Most of my clients are in the editorial field.

What new technologies have you had to master?

I have to update my knowledge on computer programs constantly. I must admit that I am not very good at that and I hire people who know about programming much more than I do.

How has your illustration changed to meet the new technologies?

For me, illustration is a lot about telling stories and transporting ideas. As I've always worked with different media, acrylic technique, or illustrations done by vector programs, my illustrations did not change that much. It is different providing illustrations for the Internet, since they have to be simpler and a lot of the texture you can still see in printed media is lost. On the other hand, you can do little animations and make your pictures move and sing, which provides a whole new palette of possibilities [compared to] a traditional illustration for a printed magazine.

I love textures and the haptic [quality] of paintings. The smell of a fresh silk-screened print is something I do not want to miss out on. So as often as possible, I try to work not digitally, but in the heavenly stink of the medium itself, and that makes me very very happy.

Otto Steininger: The Last Generation

What are the three most recent jobs you've done?

1. *A book jacket (design and illustration) for a novel for German publisher Arena*
2. *An illustration for Yale's medical magazine*
3. *A set of icons for* Mother Jones *magazine*

How much of your work is done for traditional (i.e., print) and untraditional (i.e., digital, toys, textiles, murals) media?

90 percent traditional (print) and 10 percent untraditional (animation, murals, watches).

What is the most challenging untraditional medium you've worked in?

Watches for Swatch and a mural for an election press center built by the United Nations in East Timor.

Who are your primary clients?

Magazines and newspapers. (Some of [my] more frequent repeat clients are the Wall Street Journal, American Lawyer, IP Law & Business, *and the* American.*)*

What new technologies have you had to master?

Since when? Being probably the last generation of artists to leave art school without ever having touched a computer (1990), I should of course list Illustrator and Photoshop; more recently, Flash and After Effects.

How has your illustration changed to meet the new technologies?

I only started using the computer for illustration in 1995. I used it to introduce a new style of crisp line drawings and collage elements. This approach would have been practically impossible with traditional media. The computer allowed me to do things I was dreaming of while still in art school, such as combining painted textures with crisp black-and-white drawings. For my thesis in art school, I ended up drawing with permanent pens on acetate, then putting the acetate on top of a painted or collage background, and then making a color copy of it to have it all in one piece. But I was never entirely satisfied with the results. I was waiting for Photoshop to arrive without knowing it. I also used the color copier a lot to change colors or fill backgrounds with flat colors. I really used the color copier much like a computer. But I did not change my illustration to meet new technologies; the two simply came together as if they had been waiting for one another.

Mural by Otto Steininger.

Patrick Leger: Magazines Mostly

What are the three most recent jobs you've done?

The last three projects I worked on were an op-ed piece for the New York Times, *a full-page illustration for* ESPN *magazine, and a quarter-page spot for the* Atlantic.

How much of your work is done for traditional (i.e., print) and untraditional (i.e., digital, toys, textiles, murals) media?

The majority of the work I do is for publications. When I started out a year ago, I did some T-shirt designs for a gallery in LA and some concept work for an animated film, but I've never done anything that really pushed my involvement in a project past the typical role of an illustrator.

What is the most challenging untraditional medium you've worked in?

None as of yet. Hopefully, opportunities along those lines will surface once I become a little more established.

Who are your primary clients?

I work with magazines the most frequently. Most of this work came about after I sent out my first promotional mailer in January 2008. The only publications I have worked with on multiple occasions are the New Yorker *and the* New York Times.

Patrick Leger illustration.

What new technologies have you had to master?

I know when I started out, I read multiple how-tos on scanning and the various resolutions used in publication. I already had a fairly broad working knowledge of Adobe Photoshop before I started working professionally. Occasionally, I have to work with Adobe Illustrator to do text or vector graphics for a piece. I'm not very adept at Illustrator, so that is fairly difficult. Most of my experimenting deals with scanning textures or brushwork (usually done with the physical drawing) and integrating them into compositions as composite layers [using] Photoshop. The work I do has a very short turnaround time, which doesn't foster many opportunities to investigate a lot of the higher functions of many graphics programs, but I think my work is fairly simplistic and the inclusion of more complicated digital effects might be detrimental to the look of the illustration. Most of the equipment I use is pretty standard: a Wacom tablet, a scanner, and a small laser printer.

How has your illustration changed to meet the new technologies?

Much of what I struggle with now is trying to imitate the processes and appearances of hand-done techniques through digital means. Since I have neither the facilities for printmaking processes nor the time (or room for mistakes) to paint pieces, I have to resort to constructing things piecemeal using a combination of fast-drying materials, scanning them into a Photoshop layer, and then coloring digitally. The scanned layers can then be saved and used in other pieces, which gives me an expanding library of visual devices that I can integrate into future projects. My reason for illustrating like this is probably a response to working as a student in physical mediums for so long: I have a greater attachment to their imperfections and stylistic qualities [and prefer them over] the pristine look of work that is completely digital. It almost becomes paradoxical to think that I'm trying to get away from my work looking digital by using more complex digital processes.

Randall Enos: Irreversibly Traditional

What are the three most recent jobs you've done?

1. Modern Arabian Horse *magazine (cover and three interior illustrations)*
2. *The* Milken Institute Review *(five double-page spreads, black-and-white)*
3. Rethinking Schools *(cover and inside illustration)*

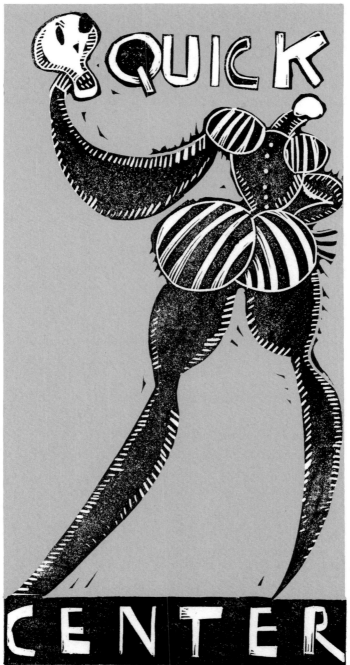

Randall Enos illustration.

How much of your work is done for traditional (i.e., print) and untraditional (i.e., digital, toys, textiles, murals) media?

I've only had one job in the last forty years or so that could be considered untraditional.

What is the most challenging untraditional medium you've worked in?

The only one I've had, really, which was a group of outdoor banners for the parking area of an arts center located at a university.

Who are your primary clients?

These days my primary clients are newspapers such as the Los Angeles Times, *the* Hartford Courant, *and the* Wall Street Journal.

What new technologies have you had to master?

None, really, except the colorization of my work using Photoshop because my traditional medium of using Pantone papers to print on has been eliminated due to the cessation of the manufacture of the papers.

How has your illustration changed to meet the new technologies?

Only in the respect that I now color my work by using the Pantone colors on Photoshop.

Rian Hughes: 15 Percent Non-Print

What are the three most recent jobs you've done?

1. *Illustrations and design for* Ugenia Lavender, *a series of six books by Geri Halliwell, published by Macmillan*
2. *Covers for* Sadie Rocks, *a series of books by Karen McCombie, published by Scholastic*
3. *Logo designs for X-Ray Kid, a games and animation start-up in LA*

How much of your work is done for traditional (i.e., print) and untraditional (i.e., digital, toys, textiles, murals) media?

Mostly still print—about 15 percent non-print.

What is the most challenging untraditional medium you've worked in?

Cycle helmet designs—figuring out how the image would distort over the dome shape and where the holes would end up.

Rian Hughes illustration.

Who are your primary clients?

Comic book publishers, music companies, and book publishers.

What new technologies have you had to master?

I have still to master FontLab, and am using Fontographer 4.1 from 1995, [which is] prehistoric in software terms. Other than that, the usual Adobe programs—InDesign, Illustrator, Photoshop.

How has your illustration changed to meet the new technologies?

I'd say it's taken advantage of the new technologies, especially in the ease [with which] one can incorporate text and image into an integrated whole.

Sam Weber: Blogging

What are the three most recent jobs you've done?

A portrait for Spin *magazine, an illustration for* Harvard Business Review, *and a cover for* DC comics.

How much of your work is done for traditional (i.e., print) and untraditional (i.e, digital, toys, textiles, murals) media?

Almost all is traditional. Every now and then, I will do something for a Web site.

Illustration by Sam Weber.

What is the most challenging untraditional medium you've worked in?

I did some concept work for an animated film last fall, which was a lot of fun, but definitely out of my comfort zone.

Who are your primary clients?

Mainly magazines and book publishers here in New York.

What new technologies have you had to master?

Does Photoshop count?

How has your illustration changed to meet the new technologies?

I've only been working for about two-and-a-half years, so I can't really say changing technology has affected it that much. I suppose the rise of blogs and illustration-specific news Web sites has affected the way I stay in touch with my peers and keep on top of what other artists and designers are doing.

Stephen Savage: Needlepoint

What are the three most recent jobs you've done?

1. *An icon for the* New York Times
2. *A spot for* IEEE Spectrum *magazine*
3. *A spot for* 5280, *a magazine in Denver*

Which of these jobs were done for a venue or medium that was untraditional (not editorial)?

All three were editorial. Editorial is still my bread and butter.

How much of your work is done for traditional (i.e., print) and untraditional (i.e., digital, toys, textiles, murals) media?

My one and only untraditional job has been children's lunchboxes called Munchlers. I've been doing some needlepoint, too, but it doesn't earn me any money.

What is the most challenging untraditional medium you've worked in?

Needlepoint is very labor-intensive, but very relaxing at the same time.

Who are your primary clients?

Editorial makes up roughly 50 percent of my income. 30 percent is children's books and 20 percent is teaching and other miscellaneous sources. I'm still very dependent on the New York Times *for steady income.*

What new technologies have you had to master?

The computer has changed my world, as it has for all illustrators. The technology is constantly changing, and I'm always struggling to keep up with the newest

Stephen Savage's lunchbox creations.

programs. Right now, my main computer is a four-year-old Mac G4 Powerbook, and it feels like a dinosaur.

How has your illustration changed to meet the new technologies?

My work, especially my editorial work, has gotten more 'computery' over the years. That's why it's important for me to continue to do things the 'old way': linocuts, sewing, etc.

Ted McGrath: Backdrops and Hand Binding

What are the three most recent jobs you've done?

My last three jobs were an op-ed illustration for the New York Times, *a half-page for* PlanSponsor *magazine, and several abstracted black-and-white panels based on Scottish tartans for* PRINT *magazine, to be used as backdrops in a photo shoot.*

What of these jobs were done for a venue or medium that was untraditional (not editorial)?

The PRINT *magazine job was definitely not what I would consider my usual type of illustration assignment.*

How much of your work is done for traditional (i.e., print) and untraditional (i.e., digital, toys, textiles, murals) media?

Only within the last year have I picked up more untraditional assignments, and they probably only account for about 25 percent or less of the work that I do (the rest being mainly editorial or advertising projects). That said, these untraditional assignments often challenge me a lot more as an illustrator and image maker and, by direct extension, usually force me to grow in some way through the process. In most cases, I'm thrilled with the results of these projects.

What is the most challenging untraditional medium you've worked in?

Last summer I was contacted by an advertising firm in Atlanta called WestWayne. They were in the midst of overhauling their methodology and operating philosophy based on friendship psychology and would be changing the name of their business to 22Squared, after the square root of the number of friends the average person has in [his or her] lifetime. I was commissioned to create a forty-page 'zine (from some light numerology-based text from one of their copy writers and the general handmade/collaged aesthetic of my sketchbooks) that would serve as a sort of manifesto or handbook to be given to employees at all levels at a relaunch party. The book had to be manufactured in-house and had to go from sketch to a finished run of 350 copies in four days. I was flown down to Atlanta from Brooklyn and given a lesser-used office/storage space a floor above the company's main office. [There, I] got to work, frantically drawing, painting, lettering, and designing the book as copy became finalized and available. Fueled by a steady flow of coffee and cheeseburgers from a nearby café, and with the help of Matthew McNerney and Sara St. Onge—the freelance designer and art director on the project, respectively—we pulled it together, hand-binding and defacing the chipboard covers hours before the books had to be distributed.

Who are your primary clients?

Several sections of the New York Times, PlanSponsor, Esquire Russia, *and* 22Squared Advertising *in Atlanta.*

Ted McGrath illustration.

What new technologies have you had to master?

I'd hardly pretend to be a master of any imaging software, as I'm continually blown away by what you can do in Photoshop or Illustrator in a few keystrokes. That said, for two other projects last year I began playing with After Effects and dabbling in some basic animation. Collaborating with Paul Weil on an installation for the 2006 College Music Journal (CMJ) festival at Galapagos in Brooklyn, we managed to come up a ten-minute looping animation to be projected on a wall over a reflective pool that was akin to the cut-paper animation from Monty Python, *though it probably wasn't as funny and I'm not sure if it made that much sense. It's definitely a venue/medium I look forward to working in on a more regular basis, and I've been trying to school myself a little more thoroughly in my spare time.*

How has your illustration changed to meet the new technologies?

I've been working more piecemeal and then assembling collages digitally, trying to fake a more 'analog' aesthetic and finish in Photoshop. This allows me to make any changes to the final art faster by adjusting the individual components without having to re-draw or re-scan large pieces of art. I also sometimes use these layered files as experiments for animations, though I'm months away from being confident enough in that stuff to show it to anyone.

Victor Juhasz: Making Oil Paintings

What are the three most recent jobs you've done?

Assignments for Rolling Stone, *the* New York Observer, *and the* Nation.

How much of your work is done for traditional (i.e., print) and untraditional (i.e., digital, toys, textiles, murals) media?

*There are any number of pieces where the primary purpose is traditional but the publications (*Sierra, Rolling Stone, *the* New York Observer*) also have Web sites where the pieces will appear as well.*

What is the most challenging untraditional medium you've worked in?

Private commissions, oil paintings; but that's not very high-tech or untraditional. It's a different frame of mind when working on the piece. [There is] less concern with deadlines and more focus on playing with the paints. I will be doing original artwork for the Air Force Art Program, a combination of reportorial (drawing and photographing on the spot during military ops) and studio work. Hopefully, [it] will achieve a you-are-there effect, but [I] have no finished work as of yet to show for it, just sketches.

Who are your primary clients?

Magazines, some newspapers, and children's books.

What new technologies have you had to master?

Nothing has been mastered. I'm still wrangling my way through Photoshop, but getting better. I don't know Illustrator or any of that great drawing tablet stuff that everyone raves about. I know some Powerpoint, but I remain very much mired in the nineteenth century. One of these days I will have to commit to paying for some private training.

How has your illustration changed to meet the new technologies?

I have for years now worked much smaller than I did starting out thirty some odd years ago. Griping from clients about difficulty [in] scanning big pieces sort of took

Illustration by Victor Juhasz.

88

the fun out of working large. Many of my pieces nowadays can fit on my tabloid scanner in a one-sweep scan. Sending hi-res digital files instead of using FedEx, which used to be thought of as fast, in one sense has made life a lot easier, in another sense more compressed, as clients assume that a twelfth-hour assignment is easier to pull off. Working smaller has definitely altered my drawing style, not always for the better. Oftentimes, the challenge is to keep the drawing loose, gestural, and feeling fresh, which working smaller can often inhibit. However, working smaller reinforces the focus on character and content in the people and less on the grand gesture.

Viktor Koen: Starting Traditional

What are the three most recent jobs you've done?
1. BusinessWeek: *illustrations on business travel that incorporated retro characters in contemporary travel situations*
2. Africa Investor *magazine cover: illustrating the fact that Africa has registered in the radar of international financial institutions (I used photos I took [for no particular reason] a few years ago of a sonar station at the Military Museum in Athens and a radar screen I shot at the Midway aircraft carrier last summer in San Diego)*
3. Media Nation: *illustration and design of the logo for an animated series pilot*

Which of these jobs were done for a venue or medium that was untraditional (not editorial)?
The logo for Media Nation's *pilot includes elements in motion suitable for the medium but also a static version for printed materials, including a companion graphic novel.*

How much of your work is done for traditional (i.e., print) and untraditional (i.e., digital, toys, textiles, murals) media?
Even though my images have been reproduced on snowboards, skateboards, and iPod covers, they were originally produced for editorial use.

What is the most challenging untraditional medium you've worked in?
The turning of an image into a belt buckle was long and tedious. Even though it was the sculptor, Eli Livingston, who did the heavy lifting

Viktor Koen's *Damsels in Armor* illustration and labor-intensive belt buckle.

(sculpting), I found the technical and production aspects nerve-wracking. The design was an intricate helmet from my Damsels in Armor series and it took about ten rounds of corrections and a few of prototyping before a series of casting adventures and finishing tests. The end result was well worth it and I proudly wear it every day, but I am not sure there is another one in my near future.

Who are your primary clients?

The New York Times, Time, Newsweek, Esquire, *Penguin, Random House, Harper Collins, Houghton Mifflin,* Wired, Men's Health, Fortune, Money, Forbes, BusinessWeek, InformationWeek, Portfolio, Billboard, Los Angeles, *Ziff Davis Media, and the* Wall Street Journal.

What new technologies have you had to master?

Since my work has been digital for the last ten years, other than following Photoshop updates, nothing drastically new has been introduced to my palette. Maybe it's because it took years to turn that program from a piece of software into an expressive tool. Maybe it's because I am lazy. Digital photography has proven to be an invaluable asset by allowing easy capture of objects and textures for my compositions, and I devote hours to photography, especially when traveling.

How has your illustration changed to meet the new technologies?

My illustrations have always been idea-based, so it was more about the technology delivering my images than my images meeting the technology. I am intrigued by motion, and After Effects can't be far for me as a first step into animation, but I see it as an extension of my core imagemaking, according to the projects at hand. If it was up to me I would rather learn carpentry than a new software.

Ward Sutton: Mostly Editorial

What are the three most recent jobs you've done?

1. *Illustration of John McCain, Larry King, and Barbara Walters in Indiana Jones garb for* Radar *magazine*
2. *Illustration of Obama, Clinton, and McCain for* MAD *magazine*
3. *T-shirt design for the Wishlist Foundation*

Which of these jobs were done for a venue or medium that was untraditional (not editorial)?

The [Wishlist Foundation] T-shirt.

How much of your work is done for traditional (i.e., print) and untraditional (i.e., digital, toys, textiles, murals) media?

The vast majority of my illustration work is traditional. However, I also am a cartoonist and animator, and last year I painted a mural.

What is the most challenging untraditional medium you've worked in?

The mural I painted last year was very satisfying and also a challenge to figure out how to transfer my illustration to a wall. I ended up getting a computer projector, hooking up my laptop, and projecting the illustration on the wall. I used the projection like a sketch, avoided using pencil or anything on the wall, and just painted directly from that. The mural was in a home, so it was kind of nerve-wracking at first, as I worried about making any mistake with the paint, but after I got going it was a lot of fun. I'd like to do more.

Who are your primary clients?

Mostly editorial.

What new technologies have you had to master?

A computer of mine died, so I was forced to upgrade and decided to go whole hog. Previously I would draw by hand, scan with Photoshop, run the image through Streamline (a now-defunct program), and finish in Illustrator 8 in Apple's 'classic' mode. With the new computer, classic mode was no longer an option. So (happily) I've been forced to get the latest Adobe Creative Suite and a Wacom tablet. With a little help I've begun working in Photoshop for my illustration work and using the Wacom, which I love. I have a regular cartoon parody I do for the Onion *(under the persona of Kelly) that I still complete in Illustrator, but otherwise I'm switching over to Photoshop.*

How has your illustration changed to meet the new technologies?

The new technologies have given me greater freedom to give more depth to my illustration by scanning in textures, photos, etc., to make my illustrations more of a mixed-media affair. Also, the Wacom tablet and Photoshop are allowing me to add shading to illustrations in a whole new way, which is exciting. The new technology will also actually allow me to work more old-school, ironically, as I plan to do some work in watercolor and other media and combine it with my ink drawing in Photoshop to create illustrations that are composites of multiple pieces of art. The way I use the computer is also prompting me to experiment and try new styles of illustration.

Wishlist foundation T-shirt designed by Ward Sutton.

Wendy Plovmand: Magazines and Labels

What are the three most recent jobs you've done?

A test illustration for a book from Organic Pharmacy, a book cover for Orion Books, and an illustration for the cover of a Danish fashion magazine.

How much of your work is done for traditional (i.e., print) and untraditional (i.e., digital, toys, textiles, murals) media?

Traditional (print) 90–95 percent
Untraditional (T-shirts, wallpaper) 5–10 percent

What is the most challenging untraditional medium you've worked in?

I wish I had done more untraditional pieces like toys, porcelain, etc. The most untraditional medium [I've worked in] so far is textiles, and that's not really untraditional anymore.

Who are your primary clients?

Magazines and fashion labels.

What new technologies have you had to master?

I like to develop and mix techniques. I use both computer-designed and handcrafted pieces.

How has your illustration changed to meet the new technologies?

I haven't changed it to meet the new technology; when I change or develop [my art], it's because I want a certain expression.

Wendy Plovmand illustration.

Chapter Four

Marketing Traditional Illustration

The editorial and publishing marketplace (magazines, newspapers, books, and to a lesser extent, advertising) continues to be a primary source of work and income for the freelance illustrator. Unlike the newer areas of toy, game, and product design, the targeted audience of the editorial or publishing art director is readily available, and the methods for reaching it are established.

This chapter will address all aspects of marketing your work to this area, including Web sites, "alternative" Web sites, e-mail blasts, and traditional "snail" mail. We will address how to find mailing lists, produce promotional material, engage in direct mail, and set up your portfolio for one or all of these media. These recommendations are based upon interviews with over one hundred practicing professionals of all ages functioning in the editorial market.

The first thing to remember is that you need to establish a presence. This means your work should be visible and accessible to the potential art buyer at all times. There are various ways of doing this, from the traditional portfolio to new digital media. We will start with the new and work our way to the old.

Building a Web Site

Your Web site is your most visible portfolio. Here are some "Dos" and "Don'ts."

- Do not be creative with the name of your site. The site should simply be your name. You are not Slim Jim or Stringbean Jim, even if your friends call you that. If an art director has seen your work in a publication or an annual, access to your Web site should be as easy as Googling your real name (unless Slim Jim *is* your real name or *nom de crayon*).
- Do hire a Webmaster to set up your site. Most illustrators with good computer skills are limited when it comes to the mechanics of setting up a site that is professional and easily manageable.
- Do not get too tricky with the bells and whistles. Unless you want to sell your services as a Web designer, the worst thing you can do is make the site more energetic than the work. The second-worst thing you can do is make it so souped-up that it crashes. Art directors hate when their computers freeze or crash, and they also have good memories.
- Do show your various assets in an intelligent and organized manner. Break down your Web site into sections, such as into "Published" and "Unpublished," or "Editorial," "Advertising," etc. If there is a series of images, make sure they are easy to access.
- Do not be inconsistent. Art directors expect consistency in craft and content in your portfolio. They want to be assured that if they assign a job to you they will have a clear idea of what you will give them in return. If, for example, you have a series of still-lifes that you love, but know they don't quite fit with your editorial work, then create a separate category titled "Still Life." The art director can open this section knowing that you acknowledge it as separate from your published portfolio.

You should definitely get help building your Web site. Since professionals can be expensive (unless they owe you a favor or you can trade their expertise for your own), it is best to locate students or recent graduates from computer arts or Web design programs—some may work simply for creative freedom, others may charge a reasonable hourly rate. Some Web creators are simply technical, while others are designers as well. Your focus should be on the selection of the work, though you might also contribute to layout and type selection.

Your Web site is a blank page. Editing is crucial. An art director should be able to maneuver your site without entering every category. For example, if you decide to set up categories like "Home," "Illustrations," "Special Projects," "Work Archive," "Fine Art," etc., make sure that each section is edited. Do not pad your categories with unimpressive work.

Let's say that again: Your portfolio should be limited to your best work, whether it is published or not.

Alternative Web Sites

In addition to your own Web site, you can join alternative or group sites as a way of reaching a broader array of art directors. Each member is given a page and individualized Web address. Buyers visit the sites to discover new artists and see new work. The feedback from illustrators we've surveyed is positive; most agree that the sites increased the traffic back to their individual Web sites. Their recommendation is to use alternative Web sites in combination with your primary Web site. Refer to the Web directory for a list of Web sites that provide services such as portfolio hosting.

Illustration Blogs

Over the past few years, many illustrators have linked individual blogs to their primary Web sites. Unlike Web sites, the blogs are interactive, allowing an interchange between illustrators through posting. This is more about communication than selling, although selling is still possible. Specific areas of the creative process can be explored on individual bases. But most importantly, illustrators across the globe can trade information of all kinds, from great finds to disastrous clients. Some blogs are more ambitious than others, and some are umbrellas for various illustrators. Increasingly, the blog is becoming the primary networking venue for illustrators.

Illustration Directories

Illustration directories charge a per-page rate. The rates vary based upon size, color, and distribution. The directories are distributed to art directors and buyers in printed form. Many directories also include exposure on their Web sites. The majority of directories are not juried, although most reserve the right to decline illustrators with unsuitable work. Here is a selection of directories:

THE BLACK BOOK: *The Black Book* is the most recognized resource for creative buyers worldwide—it is a comprehensive collection of recent work from top illustrators in the creative community.

WORKBOOK ILLUSTRATION ANNUAL: First published in 1978, the *Workbook* remains the most used sourcebook in the creative industry. *Workbook*, distributed throughout the US and Canada and sold all over Europe and Asia, provides the world's leading advertising agencies, corporations, and design firms with a carefully selected guide to discovering top creative talent.

3×3 ILLUSTRATION DIRECTORY: Featuring the selected work from it annual ProShow as well as recent gallery and showcase artists, the *3×3 Illustration Directory* is distributed free of charge to 4,400 leading art directors, art buyers, and graphic designers in Connecticut, New York, and New Jersey. Page rates are the lowest of any directory because, as publisher Charles Hively says, "We wanted to reward those who have supported the magazine by keeping the page rates so low. And being a very selective directory, we're unique. It's almost like a curated show, rather than a book of ads."

Illustration Annuals

All annuals are juried. Entry fees vary. If accepted, there may be additional costs for hanging in competition exhibitions. Annuals are printed and sold through bookstores or promotional sites. When you are listed in an annual, your work appears with other work chosen by a jury of professionals. Unlike directories, the annuals are not distributed to art directors free of charge, but art directors know that a pre-selection process has taken place. See the Web index for a list of the most popular annuals.

Mailing Lists and Self-Promotion

The number one rule regarding mailing lists of art directors is, Do not buy one. The mailing list, which often includes more than five thousand art directors, is of little use if you have no idea who these people are and what kind of art they buy. There are a few ways of developing your own list of editorial art directors. Go to a bookstore or library with a pencil and paper. Spend as long as it takes to look through every magazine in each thematic category. Every magazine has what is called a *masthead*, usually within the first few pages. The masthead lists the address of the magazine and the names of art directors and editors. Write this information down—it is called harvesting sources.

If this process is too tedious, there is a Web site dedicated to editorial mastheads. For a reasonable fee (around $24 per year), you can log in and view the mastheads of thousands of magazines. Here's the Web site's advertisement:

··

MASTHEADS.org SUBJECT INDEX
[Login/password required for database access.]
Need a Contact at a Publication NOT Listed Here?
We probably have a contact. Ask us!

Mastheads.org Access Options
Get 500 + magazine staff mastheads all in one online directory!
Complete, unabridged staff lists with information on how to contact editors and magazine staffers—at your fingertips anytime, anywhere.

··

You can also harvest art directors' contacts from annuals, though it can be tedious. Every annual includes a comprehensive list of the names, addresses, and e-mails of illustrators, art directors, magazines, and companies. Going through the annuals allows you to see illustrations that were bought by specific art directors the year before. Unfortunately, the address of the art director is not listed. Your list of magazines can be cross-referenced with mastheads for mailing addresses.

Getting Art Directors to Visit Your Web Site

You now have a list of art directors and mailing addresses of magazines that you feel will relate to your work. The first step in getting an art director interested enough to go to your Web site is by mailing samples of your work. E-mailing a sample and a link to the site is fine, but it is not a substitute for a physical card or flyer.

The card or flyer should contain at least four samples on a postcard printed with your name, Web site, phone number, and e-mail and snail mail addresses somewhere prominent. Cards or flyers can be printed out on your computer (using good paper stock). Postcard printing has become quite reasonable, but you will still end up with a quantity that exceeds your mailing list. Printing your own cards or flyers also allows you to customize each packet to suit the art director or client.

Most illustrators send two mailings per year.

Promotion Options

We've provided some basic advice for promoting your illustration. But since illustrators are a creative lot, it stands to reason that you can also devise your own promotional options. Honestly, if everyone followed the same fundamental principles, everyone's promotion could look the same, and since the first goal of promotion is to attract attention—to rise above the crowd—the more unique or novel the promotion, the better chance there is of capturing an art director's or client's eye.

The options run wide—everything from interactive videos to animations, from customized books to toys and games. There is nothing better for your cause than a promotion that cannot be thrown away; but this, of course, demands an understanding of what people want. An original print is harder to throw away than a mass-produced anything. But a terrifically clever mass-produced object can be just the thing an art director will put on his or her wall or shelf. When marketing yourself, be as creative and talented as you want your prospective client to think you are.

Twenty Ways to Get Work

We asked illustrators their best way to get assignments. The following twenty are compiled from one hundred responses. (Not surprisingly, many of the methods are similar.)

1. Call to make appointments with every art director or art buyer whose name you can find and who will see you (don't call blind: make sure you have a person's name).
2. Network: go to designer events and meet as many designers as possible. They often need illustrators, so follow up with e-mails.
3. Make it a point to befriend older illustrators. The ones you meet may be extraordinarily generous in introducing you to potential clients.
4. Self-publish a book of your drawings and send it to a select list of clients.
5. Do hand-lettering. Combining illustration and design seems to increase options.

6. Put advertisements in some of the showcase books.

7. Get an artist's representative.

8. Initiate projects on your own (commercial and fine art) that will get noticed by art buyers.

9. Enter as many competitions as possible that are visible to art directors.

10. Go to American Illustration's annual party. Aside from being an exhibition of work, it is a good way to meet other illustrators and exchange ideas.

11. Spend a great deal of time at the Barnes & Noble magazine rack. Without editing, go through every magazine to see what kind of illustrations they are commissioning.

12. Attend seminars in special areas like children's book illustration. You will make good contacts not only with art directors but with editors as well.

13. Bring a sketchbook and draw everywhere you go. You will be amazed at how many contacts you'll make this way.

14. Send oversized digital prints to galleries instead of slides or CDs. The response will be much better if they are actually holding a print.

15. Stay in touch with the friends you made during graduate school. Meet on a weekly basis to continue a group discussion about your work.

16. If successful illustrators and art directors come to a class you are taking to give lectures, hand them promo pieces and ask if you can contact them by phone.

17. Always include a hand-written note when you send promo pieces. Include a comment specific to the art director.

18. Also include a hand-written note when you are included in an updated mailing list.

19. Chip in with friends and buy a table at the MoCCA art festival. Even if you are not a cartoonist, you will made good contacts with art directors who are interested in storytelling.

20. Wishing never works; make sure to send out multiple portfolios and follow up with e-mails and printed promotional pieces.

Selecting an Artist's Representative

For many young and veteran illustrators in traditional and new media, working with an artist's representative (a "rep" or "agent") is the best way to market work and have enough time at the end of the day to actually do the work.

Hawking your own wares is time-consuming and sometimes ego-deflating. It can also be hit-or-miss. A good rep knows the right places to pitch your work and the best art directors and art buyers to approach, so it is useful to consider this method, even if only for a certain segment of your work. Here are ten pointers to keep in mind:

1. Reps will either take you on exclusively or in part. Be certain when exploring your options to determine what the best strategy is.

2. Reps sometimes specialize in particular media. Some may only do editorial, others editorial and advertising. Some only do merchandise, while others might only handle children's books.

3. Reps are interested in assets they can sell. Most reps are not interested in your experimentation. If you want to experiment and want a rep, it's best to keep it to yourself until both you and the rep can agree it is salable.

4. Reps are in business to make money—for you *and* them. Be prepared to give them anywhere from 10 to 25 percent of what you earn.

5. Reps want to promote your work, but you are often asked to pay for the promotion. Don't be surprised if all a rep will do for you is take your work around to prospective clients—the rest is on your shoulders.

6. Reps should not have a say in your style or content, but sometimes they will try to get involved. Be certain to establish boundaries between art and commerce.

7. A rep can be your friend, but don't ever forget this is a business relationship; do not rely on a rep to massage your ego or insecurities, unless you are quite profitable.

8. Reps represent more people than just you. Remember, while they will represent you in good faith, not all their clients are equal. If you make them money, they will shower more attention on you.

9. Reps are not always your best representative. Many art directors and art buyers want to know the artist, not the rep. So after they've made a sale, develop your own relationship with your client.

10. Reps are nothing without you. They are selling your work, so make sure they understand what it is you do, and what you want to get out of being an illustrator.

Chapter Five

Working in New Media

It occurrs to us that many younger illustrators go straight from school into untraditional genres. Fashion, toys, and animation are decidedly alluring to many young artists today. The computer has made working in film and product design easier to engage. However, we were fascinated to find that many respondents were working in "conventional" ways (with their hands) and in common genres. But there were a number of respondents who said they were either branching out into untraditional media or starting their own from scratch. When asked what the new technologies have offered them and how have they changed their working habits, the response was almost universal: "These are the media we grew up with; we haven't changed."

James Jean: No Editorial Assignments, Please

What are the three most recent jobs you've done?

I created murals for the Prada epicenter stores in New York and Los Angeles, as well for their runway show in Milan. These graphics were applied to all the clothing, bags, accessories, and shoes for the Prada Spring/Summer 2008 collection.

Additionally, I wrote, storyboarded, and designed an animated film based on visual cues from the murals. The design agency, 2 × 4, applied designs from the film to all Prada stores and windows worldwide.

The Grateful Palate commissioned three triptychs to adorn high-end wines (nine labels total).

I am currently creating two posters for TBWA-Chiat Day Paris for the organization AIDES.

Which of these jobs were done for a venue or medium that was untraditional (not editorial)?

All of them in some way, but the posters for AIDES will be used in an advertising capacity to encourage the use of condoms among the youth of France.

How much of your work is done for traditional (i.e., print) and untraditional (i.e., digital, toys, textiles, murals) media?

I haven't accepted any editorial assignments for almost two years, but I continue to create one cover per month for DC's Vertigo comics. Any other work I accept is usually untraditional.

What is the most challenging untraditional medium you've worked in?

Film and motion is perhaps the most challenging. I've also worked with Motion Theory on some commercials for Cadillac and McDonald's—I designed characters, environments, textures, and color palettes to be interpreted in a 3-D virtual world.

Who are your primary clients?

Right now, I'm mainly selling my original artwork and prints online.

What new technologies have you had to master?

Since graduating from art school, I've had to learn Photoshop and a bit of Web design.

How has your illustration changed to meet the new technologies?

I think my work is constantly evolving, so new technologies inform my work in different ways. Sometimes, my work is a reaction to the prevalent methods of working.

Top: James Jean's illustration for Prada. Bottom: The illustration applied to a building.

Jeremyville: Multi Multi

What are the three most recent jobs you've done?

I was commissioned by Converse US to design a shoe for their 100 RED project. The shoe [came] out in October 2008. It is a pink, red, and black leather Chuck Taylor shoe, and was launched recently in LA. Rossignol in Utah and France commissioned me to design some snowboards and apparel for their new range. I have also been commissioned to design various toys and apparel for Kidrobot in New York.

Which of these jobs were done for a venue or medium that was untraditional (not editorial)?

The thinking is more multi-disciplinary, and not just a flat, traditional, editorial illustration. Rather, it takes into account factors such as functionality of the object, style trends in the marketplace, innovation, and what is cool right now.

I worked for three years as an illustrator for the Sydney Morning Herald, *Australia's leading newspaper, and there the brief was to convey a message—to add something to the dialogue of the article in as concise a manner as possible so the reader could grasp the message quickly. This was a totally different mindset from the work I now create in illustration, which I feel is more challenging.*

Once I felt I had mastered the realm of editorial illustration, I needed to push myself further as an artist. I know some artists are happy to continue working in one field, such as editorial for a newspaper, but I needed further challenges, and I take those skill sets with me to the next genre of art I pursue.

I still enjoy the concept of conveying a message or story in an illustration, but I now have my comic stories that fulfill that purpose for me. [They are] silent haiku vignettes that paint a moment or feeling, for the reader to add [his or her] own circumstance and memory to complete the story's atmosphere and message.

How much of your work is done for traditional (i.e., print) and untraditional (i.e., digital, toys, textiles, murals) media?

I'd say about 90 percent for non-traditional media, however, I'm currently writing this from Rome, and just today met with the editor of the largest magazine on music and lifestyle, XL magazine, *in Italy, which is also an insert in* La Repubblica *(a newspaper). The editor is featuring me in a regular comic story section within the magazine, which has a print run of 400,000 copies. It feels good to harken back to my days at the* Sydney Morning Herald *and the smell of printing ink.*

Converse All-Star shoes designed by Jeremyville.

I visited the XL *offices in Rome, which reminded me very much of any editorial office in any newspaper worldwide. They seem to have a similar, very real and honest atmosphere, something very much at the coal face. Newspapers feel like an honest day's work.*

I remember drawing at the Sydney Morning Herald *in the afternoon, then picking up the paper from the newsstand in the early morning on the way home. I loved the immediacy of that art form.*

What is the most challenging untraditional medium you've worked in?

Toy design, for the length of development, and complexity in translating a 2-D concept successfully into 3-D. I have a degree in architecture from Sydney University, and [I] feel at ease thinking spatially and in the built form, so I think that training has helped me in the toy genre.

Who are your primary clients?

Converse, Kidrobot, Rossignol, Zoo York, Tiger Beer, IdN Publishers, MTV Italy, Nickelodeon UK, Colette Paris, Upper Playground, Corbis, Graniph T-shirts (Japan).

What new technologies have you had to master?

Dreamweaver MX, the art of schmoozing in the twenty-first century, enduring several 'round-the-world plane trips a year to meet with clients, Flash, and new languages to interact on a human level with overseas clients.

How has your illustration changed to meet the new technologies?

For me, when I now put pen to paper, I contemplate several incarnations that the drawing might take. It could become a T-shirt, a toy, or a repeat pattern on a fabric—the outcome of the drawing could have several possibilities.

Sometimes I will, of course, create a design specifically for a medium in mind; however, I generally find it more fun to simply draw in my sketchbook, then choose a specific design for a specific medium from this vast pool of sketchbook work. That keeps the work fresh, and keeps me entertained, and in that way it does not feel like work, it feels more like play. To me, that's the key to continually challenging yourself and growing and inventing. A simple black pen and a blank sketchbook is the starting point for almost everything.

Lin Wilson: Iconographics

What are the three most recent jobs you've done?

1. *ICON LANGUAGE: We created icons for Eastman Kodak's Graphic Communication Group to communicate products and services to an international audience for an upcoming trade show in Germany.*
2. *INSTRUCTIONAL MANUAL: We worked with the New York agency Bandujo and the New Jersey Motor Vehicle Commission to visualize key rules of the road for a revamp of their driving manual.*
3. *INFOGRAPHICS FOR DIRECT MAIL: We created an infographic to explain a records management company to their customers. Using a postcard, our graphic provided a bird's eye view of their complex offering.*

Which of these jobs were done for a venue or medium that was untraditional (not editorial)?

From instructions on packaging to Web site icons, our work has high utility to work across any and all media. As an early adopter of Adobe Illustrator, I honed the process of making small icons. Translating that thinking to larger illustrations and infographics has been natural and necessary as most of our work tends to be used in untraditional ways.

ICON LANGUAGE: The icons will be used in very broad ways, including trade show signage, PowerPoint, print collateral, and Web sites. This put an emphasis on clarity of message and artwork, since they are used as big as a large poster and as small as a pixel-based icon (on the Web site).

INSTRUCTIONAL MANUAL: The infographics for the driving manual will be used in a print booklet for the general public and also as an online, PDF-based document. Because our illustration visualizes non-verbal information, this assignment demonstrated how we could communicate concepts [that are] not easily put into text. This also fit in with a new need for multilingual communications that require less text to be translated and more information to be communicated by universally understood visual concepts.

INFOGRAPHICS FOR DIRECT MAIL: This is untraditional in that it was the main image in a direct mail campaign and provided in one glance the physical infrastructure of the business as well as their services. This project demonstrated how efficient the infographic could be in bending reality to fit all of the ingredients into one bird's eye view.

What is the most challenging untraditional medium you've worked in?

It would have to be PowerPoint presentations. Many of them look awful, since they are never really designed. These slide-shows contain some our client's core messaging in a clip art wrapper. It's actually quite easy to design a superficial makeover, but much more challenging to create great design that communicates the message while avoiding typical presentation clichés. In other words, you have to avoid the tendency of the software to direct your decisions, and everyone knows how bad PowerPoint can get.

Who are your primary clients?

Advertising agencies, editorial magazines, public relations firms, and direct clients including Eastman Kodak, Draft FCB, John Wick Homes, Texas Monthly, Hanley Wood, *and Crispin Porter + Bogusky.*

What new technologies have you had to master?

We create the artwork with Adobe Illustrator, and even though we have been using it since the early '90s, we have to keep up to date with each release. For

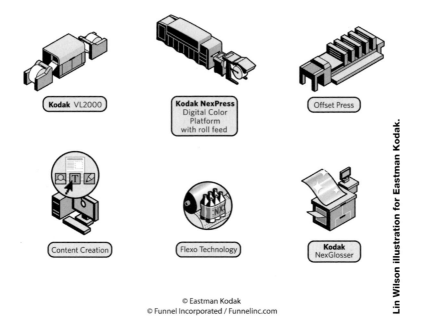

Kodak VL2000

Kodak NexPress
Digital Color
Platform
with roll feed

Offset Press

Content Creation

Flexo Technology

Kodak
NexGlosser

© Eastman Kodak
© Funnel Incorporated / Funnelinc.com

Lin Wilson illustration for Eastman Kodak.

project management, we learned how to use a Basecamp Web site, which allows us to manage the project from sketch to final art through a Web interface, and this allows us to manage client input and approvals in an efficient way.

How has your illustration changed to meet the new technologies?

It is much more precise and technical in its final form, since our work is delivered as a vector-based Illustrator file. But this fits really well with infographics, as they are very information-heavy and rely on a calculated balance of artwork, line weight, typography, and color.

Mark Marek: 1 Percent Print

What are the three most recent jobs you've done?

1. *Compositing and animation for* The Jefferson, *a.k.a.* A Young Person's Guide to History *for Adult Swim (Cartoon Network)*
2. *Character design and animation for the pilot* Deer Mike *for The Disney Channel*
3. *Comic strip for* Le Monde Diplomatique

Which of these jobs were done for a venue or medium that was untraditional (not editorial)?

[The first two] were for television and Web exposure; all of my work is digital.

How much of your work is done for traditional (i.e., print) and untraditional (i.e., digital, toys, textiles, murals) media?

All of my work is digital for digital release. Probably 1 percent is for print... most [is] for television and Web.

What is the most challenging untraditional medium you've worked in?

On a comparative basis, no particular medium has stood out as more challenging than another.

Who are your primary clients?

Television, broadcast, and film—MTV (Viacom), Cartoon Network, and various independents.

What new technologies have you had to master?

Digital animation, drawing, recording, editing, working with the Cintiq (Wacom) drawing tablet.

How has your illustration changed to meet the new technologies?

If anything, the style or line has become more clean by the inherent virtue of digital media, although some might not label it a virtue.

Melinda Beck: Slow Animation

What are the three most recent jobs you've done?

1. *Animated station ID for Nickelodeon/Noggin*
2. *An illustration for a exhibition in Ireland that teaches people about what illustration is*
3. *Gift cards for Target*

Which of these jobs were done for a venue or media that was untraditional (not editorial)?

They all were.

How much of your work is done for traditional (i.e., print) and untraditional(i.e., digital, toys, textiles, murals) media?

A few years ago, I would have said 80 percent editorial, 20 percent non-traditional; now the opposite is true.

What is the most challenging untraditional medium you've worked in?

Animation because it is so time-consuming. A sixty-second animation can take me two weeks to complete.

Who are your primary clients?

Nickelodeon/Noggin, Chronicle Books, Asset International Publications, the New York Times, Target, and Ronn Campisi Design.

What new technologies have you had to master?

I actually have not had to master any, at least not all at one time. I went to Rhode Island School of Design (RISD) in 1985, which was a year after the first Macs

Melinda Beck illustration.

were sold, and I have been using the Mac computers ever since. I have learned new techniques as the technology has changed and developed. I now create all of my work in Illustrator, Photoshop, and InDesign. I also create parts of the work using traditional techniques and then scan them into Photoshop.

How has your illustration changed to meet the new technologies?

When doing animation, the dimensions of time and sound have been added, and the idea can slowly reveal itself as the animation proceeds. When working on images for the Web, I try to create work that is simple and bold because the resolution is so low.

Patrick Dorian: Entertainment Industry

What are the three most recent jobs you've done?

1. *I created designs and illustrations used for a stop-motion-animated McDonald's UK commercial.*
2. *I storyboarded, designed, and animated two stop-motion-animated station IDs for Fangoria TV.*
3. *I created concept artwork for a video game development company.*

Still from a stop-motion animation by Patrick Dorian.

How much of your work is done for traditional (i.e., print) and untraditional (i.e., digital, toys, textiles, murals) media?

I would have to say 90 percent of my work is done for untraditional media. I might draw or sculpt something traditionally, but it all gets scanned into the computer eventually.

What is the most challenging untraditional medium you've worked in?

Animation has been the most challenging untraditional medium for me. There is a lot of work that goes into it. If you don't like to work, you won't enjoy animation. Some projects can last two weeks or even six months. Often you have to work with a team of other artists under very tight deadlines. No project is ever the same and every project has its challenges. I've had to learn about the process of animation as well as the principles of animation. I've had to really study character animation and become an illustrator/actor.

Who are your primary clients?

Directors, animation studios, music bands, and video game companies are my primary clients.

What new technologies have you had to master?

I had to learn Adobe Flash, After Effects, Photoshop, Illustrator, and Stop-Motion Pro.

How has your illustration changed to meet the new technologies?

Technology has given me very powerful tools to help me explore and promote my personal artistic vision. With all the advancements in new technology, I no longer see my illustrations bound to only the printed page. If you can draw, you can animate. Having programs such as Flash, After Effects, and Stop-Motion Pro so accessible makes it that much easier to breathe life into [my] illustrations. I can take one of my drawings or sculptures and turn them into a short film while sitting in my tiny New York apartment, without the aid of a large studio or huge budget. Your only limitation is your imagination.

Patrick Morgan: Printing on Fabric

What are the three most recent jobs you've done?

1. Vodafone mobile phones: advertising billboard and Web banner
2. Annual Report for Capital and Regional: 15 dps illustrations
3. The Daily Telegraph: *illustration of David Hockney*

Patrick Morgan illustration.

Which of these jobs were done for a venue or media that was untraditional (not editorial)?

Most of my recent jobs seem to be non-editorial: either corporate reports and advertising. The editorial work varies; sometimes [there are] plenty [of jobs] there are and then just a few.

How much of your work is done for traditional (i.e., print) and untraditional (i.e., digital, toys, textiles, murals) media?

Most of my work is print, but I have started to do a lot of large-format work like murals for bars and a wallboarding for Coca-Cola headquarters.

What is the most challenging untraditional medium you've worked in?

Printing on fabric seems to be the most challenging when trying to get a high-quality output. Screen printing varies according to the printmaker. [It is] not challenging for me, [but it] just [depends on] the skills of the printmaker.

Who are your primary clients?

My clients change constantly [because] in the UK, companies follow trends, so [they] don't really keep artists for too long. I had a regular piece in the Independent on Saturday.

What new technologies have you had to master?

I started as a screen printer, and due to tight deadlines and image color management, I have really tried to understand my digital printer (I am an image colorist for HP; a beta tester for large-format printers). [I am] finally using all the Adobe software (Photoshop, Illustrator, etc.).

How has your illustration changed to meet the new technologies?

My illustrations haven't changed too much as I have tried to apply traditional media to my work. [I am] trying to keep that screen-printed, flat-color look. Computers are good for time and [for] getting good color reproduction.

Stefan Bucher: Making Web Monsters

What are the three most recent jobs you've done?

The three most recent illustration jobs I've done are a Daily Monster mural in Seward, Nebraska, an illustrated poster advertising short-run digital printing for Typecraft Wood & Jones in Pasadena, California, and my book 100 Days of Monsters.

Which of these jobs were done for a venue or medium that was untraditional (not editorial)?

All of them.

Stefan Bucher with his life-size monster standee.

How much of your work is done for traditional (i.e., print) and untraditional (i.e., digital, toys, textiles, murals) media?

About half of my illustration work grows out of my graphic design practice, which is almost entirely print-based. The other half involves a lot of work that starts on the Web—on Dailymonster.com in particular—and later grows tendrils into posters, magazines, and other print applications.

What is the most challenging untraditional medium you've worked in?

I licensed a few of my hybrid animal illustrations to Honda for an online banner campaign last year. My drawings are quite intricate. Scaling them down to a few hundred pixels while still retaining their character was difficult.

A few weeks ago I made one of my monsters into a five-and-a-half-foot standee with a rearrangeable magnetic face. We used a digital router on half-inch PVC to get a standee that would hold up for a few consecutive high-traffic events, Comic-Con being first on the list. The process made it necessary to reduce the complexity of the blown ink lines significantly. As they usually are, they wouldn't be too fine for the router to cut, but they'd snap off at the slightest stress, like a kid pulling on one of the hairs. As with the online banners, the challenge was to reduce the complexity of the original without sacrificing the identifiable vibe of the creature.

Who are your primary clients?

At this point, my primary clients are schools and creative businesses, including ad agencies, book publishers, printers, film production companies, and art galleries.

What new technologies have you had to master?

For the monster work I had to learn a little bit of animation software (Anime Studio 5 in particular) as well as Adobe After Effects. But that's all just mixing and mastering stuff. My main challenge is still and will always be to draw better.

How has your illustration changed to meet the new technologies?

My one real concession to technology is that all my drawings are either 8½ × 11 or smaller, or are assembled from 8½ × 11 elements so that I can do my own scanning.

Yumi Heo: Making Toys

What are the three most recent jobs you've done?

My three most recent jobs were children's books. However, I have been working on designing my own line of children's gardening toys using the characters from one of my books, The Green Frogs. *John Deere is interested in this line. The other project I am working on is designing my own line of plush toys.*

Which of these jobs were done for a venue or medium that was untraditional (not editorial)?

As for the gardening toy line, I manipulate the images from my book digitally and put them on toys like watering cans, basins, water buckets, and gardening tools.

How much of your work is done for traditional (i.e., print) and untraditional (i.e., digital, toys, textiles, murals) media?

For my plush toys, I sew fabrics to create the shapes of the toys and then dip them in a rubber paint. I then paint my designs on the rubberized surface.

What is the most challenging untraditional medium you've worked in?

The most challenging medium was working with the rubber paint. It is a paint used for coating the handles of tools.

Who are your primary clients?

My plush toys [have] not [yet been] picked up yet by a company, though FAO Schwarz was so interested in them that they actually had a company in China produce samples of my plush toy line. Unfortunately, it did not work out.

What new technologies have you had to master?

I did not need any new technologies or new media. I work traditionally. However, I have had to learn how to manipulate my art digitally and transfer it to unconventional products such as metal pails, plush dolls, and T-shirts and fabrics.

How has your illustration changed to meet the new technologies?

I feel the main change for me is not in the art techniques of illustration as much as it is in my notion that illustrators must shift their target market from conventional editorial illustration to children's book illustration and the licensing of merchandise based on their illustrations such as dolls, toys, games, clothing, and other products.

My illustration for the children's book has not changed either.

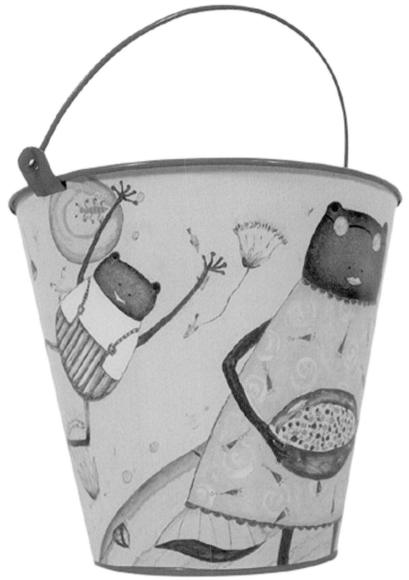

Bucket designed by Yumi Heo.

Chapter Six

Marketing the New Illustration

Over two decades ago, designers had to live in the same locale in which they worked. Because of deadlines, it was crucial for the illustrator to live in the near vicinity or cluster of publishing activity. For example, New York houses numerous book and magazine publishers and advertising and theatrical agencies. Los Angeles is the heart of the movie business and the entertainment industry. Illustrators, in order to survive, needed to live in the community to fully market themselves. Federal Express changed that. With the advent of overnight couriers, illustrators like Gary Kelly (Iowa), Anita Kunz (Toronto), William King (North Carolina), and Mark Summers (Canada) no longer needed to reside in close proximity to the geographical work locations in order to function. Even before FedEx, marketing could be accomplished through the mail, annuals, or agents who operated within the cluster, but the service made it so much faster and easier.

Prior to the Internet, when we talked about marketing, we were talking about two different things: the ability to create work from any location and the ability to market the work through existing channels. Phones and faxes are designed to facilitate two-way conversations. In the editorial marketplace, this works fine. One-on-one communication with an art director continues to be a direct channel for work.

The question is, What happens when the illustrator reaches beyond the editorial market and produces products outside the traditional definition of what an illustrator does?

We are living in a highly technological time. More than ever, there is a remarkable increase in our ability to share information and in career outlets. The freelance illustrator, previously defined as a loner, is going to have to join a group in order to market himself or herself and his or her ideas effectively. This uncharted territory demands a rethinking of the market plan in new, often daunting ways. It is necessary to understand issues of intellectual property and copyright, as well as to know good contacts and venues in which to expose the work, and this requires a network of many. It is now possible for individuals to contribute to a group without requiring a company president or art director. The practice of sharing information is skyrocketing and will continue to do so.

If you have designed a toy, game, or character, you can Google information sites and make direct contact with groups already engaged in marketing. Information about manufacturing, distribution, and prototyping is readily available in all areas. Getting things done is no longer the property of the few—it is becoming communal property.

Most illustrators consider themselves outside the group. This is understandable, considering that the illustrator has been conditioned to develop a personal style, a personal approach to problem solving, a personal approach to how he or she visualizes the world, and a personal approach to marketing what he or she does. This makes it particularly difficult for illustrators to form and sustain a group, but it has also inspired new ways to form groups.

Self-Assembly

For the illustrator, functioning without an art director, editor, and publishing house would not have been possible ten years ago. Operating without managerial direction means understanding that our electronic networks have enabled the individual to join collaborative groups with shared interests.

Toy and game conventions, comics, graphic novels, and self-publishing conventions are prevalent. For a reasonable fee, tables can be rented by individuals or groups to display individual efforts. The conventions are microcosms of what is happening on the Internet. Publishers, manufacturers, artists, and interested parties are replacing the clusters once housed in specific locales. Because sharing creates the fewest demands on the participants, illustrators are using the groups as available resources without the overlay of management.

This has, of course, opened the floodgates for work—often amateurish—that is driven by ambition to make money. Every celebrity and housewife in America is writing a children's book. Merely having a child is not necessarily the only prerequisite for being able to write a good children's book. Taking a couple of continuing-education classes in greeting cards will not usually equip you for a profitable career in the business, no matter how much marketing savvy you can muster.

Marketing Your Mother: an Arisman Tale

After my father died, my mother's only source of income was Social Security. Being independent and adamant that she live alone, she refused any money offered by me. When I sent her $50, she sent me $50 back.

On my annual Christmas visit, I saw a crèche (manger) she had made out of bread dough. Among the wise men, donkeys, manger, and Mary was a flock of sheep that were folk art masterpieces covered in wool with painted eyes and feet. I showed them to a friend who bought folk art for the Smithsonian gift shops. The flock sold out within a week. My mother accepted the check. I swung into action with a marketing plan that included letterheads, tags, package design, invoice pads, and the possibility of creating life-size pieces for the gallery market.

The Smithsonian ordered five hundred more sheep. Proud of my marketing skills, I called my mother to see how production was going. "Don't ever interfere with my life again," she said angrily. "I am so sick of making these damn sheep I could scream!" She, having a strong work ethic, completed the order, but never made anything again. I killed the creative spirit in my own mother by marketing her.

The Cart Before the Horse

There is no sure-fire recipe for success. Every working system is a mix of timing and audience response. Marcel Duchamp said, "The artist does not create alone, the spectator brings the work in contact with the external world by deciphering and interpreting its inner qualifications and thus adds his or her contribution to the creative act."

Whatever form the illustrator's creation takes outside the traditional role of illustration, it must offer some value higher than novelty in order to succeed.

We are all well aware of novelty and the fact that marketing can, on occasion, *create* a market. Remember the Pet Rock craze? Ordinary rocks, skillfully packaged and marketed, sold for $5 apiece and made millions. The advent of digital technologies have had and continue to have a direct effect on how we approach the market.

The temptation for the illustrator/entrepreneur is to think like a market researcher instead of an artist, to function as a problem-solver without a personal base. What we have to offer is a clear understanding and a leap of faith that if we develop ourselves as artists, there will be something of higher value to market than a Pet Rock. Our vision can be related to a larger audience; that can be marketed.

Thinking as an artist, Not as a Market Researcher

Professor Sir Cyril Burt, in an introduction for Arthur Koestler's book, *The Act of Creation*, said, "From time immemorial the gift of creativity has been venerated almost as if it were divine." Most artists in all fields were told by their parents that they got their talent from an uncle, grandfather, or cousin, and that this special gift was passed on through the bloodstream or by some mystical force. That belief, while intriguing, is not the whole story. Illustrators are a novel synthesis of figurative artists trained both technically and mentally to respond to text in written form. This phenomenon, in which an entire profession is tied at the hip with the publishing industry—and until recently, dependent upon it for primary income—is both complex and simple. Now that the shifts in the field have necessitated the illustrator's re-examination of his or her role, the larger issue of creativity needs to refocused.

Illustrators' skills, such as drawing and painting, tend to become more or less automatized, pre-set routines that identify a consistency in style. This is partly due to a marketplace in which changes in so-called style have not been welcomed. For the illustrator, playing by the rules means: give them what they expect, meet the deadline, and don't shift too many gears.

To quote Arthur Koestler, a British novelist, journalist, and critic:

We learn by assimilating experiences and grouping them into ordered schemata, into stable patterns of unity in variety. They enable us to cope with events and situations by applying the rules of the game appropriate to them. Habits have varying degrees of flexibility; if often repeated under unchanging conditions in a monotonous environment, they tend to become rigid and automatized.

There are two ways of escaping our more or less automatized routines of thinking and behaving. The first, of course, is the plunge into dreaming or a dream-like state, in which the codes of rational thinking are suspended. The other way is also an escape—from boredom, stagnation, intellectual predicaments, and emotional frustration—but an escape in the opposite direction; it is signaled by the spontaneous flash of insight which shows a familiar situation or event in a new light, and elicits a new response to it.

Put simply, this means that the illustrator must take charge, accept the responsibility for his or her own subject matter, and understand that a familiar situation can be drawn, painted, and written in a new light.

Words From the Wise

Daniel Hyun Lim, a.k.a. Fawn Fruits:

I got my first start in illustration not from the New York Times *or* Rolling Stone, *but from MySpace (http://www.myspace.com). We live in a cyber age and, although the methods of dropping off a portfolio have still got [their] perks, promoting oneself on the Web is enormously more rewarding. My alter-ego, Fawn Fruits, is a Web site (http://www.fawnfruits.com) dedicated to promoting my personal work, in which I am selling [thousands of] drawings for $100 each. [I credit] 95 percent of my exposed success to a strong online profile.*

John Hendrix:

It took me years to understand the difference between style and voice. Style may be [an] aesthetic decision, but your voice is what will set you apart from others. Voice is a point of view. Voice is visual thinking; cultivating your own sense of the world and how your images reflect that view is essential. Beyond the making of images, though, is authoring your own content. There is no better way to be in charge of your career than to be your own ideal art director. Set up projects and write subject matter that tells the stories that you love. Don't chase demographics and market trends. I drew and painted and collaged and tried everything under the sun searching for something that looked like I thought it should. All the time, my voice was hiding right under my nose, in the pages of my sketchbooks. I went back to a basic love of drawing and my work [started] to become what it is now [because I] rediscovered what brought me joy. From there, I made the kind of work I wanted to continue to make, regardless of whether it was marketable. The Internet is a revolution for artists because it empowers the minority: Your market will find you. Even if your following is small, the so-called long tail of the Internet allows artists who make niche work to support themselves. A career in illustration no longer depends on a majority audience.

Yuko Shimizu:

It is an exciting period for new illustrators. With Web sites and the Internet, there are no more borders in the market: [the] world is your market! But of course it means you have more competitors than ever all over the world. It is important now, more than ever, to have your personal voice [show] through in the works on your portfolio site, so possible clients remember your work among millions of Web sites [they've seen].

Nora Krug:

The field of editorial illustration has been shrinking rapidly for the last ten years, and illustrators today can't afford to subscribe themselves to just one area or medium. It is crucial for the current generation of illustrators to redefine what illustration means and can mean. New areas have emerged and expanded into commercial fields, and illustrators today work as graphic novelists, gallery artists, animators, toy designers, or game designers, developing their own personal forms of expression. What's most important is to focus on your idea, on what you want to express emotionally and intellectually. Content has become more important than medium, and illustrators don't just respond to given themes anymore. Exposing your work online is crucial because it is the most public platform. Most art directors contact me because they see my work online.

Paul Hoppe:

There are hardly any professions where it is more common to have your own Web site. Every illustration student has a Web site already. For an illustrator, it's essential. This way, a portfolio is always accessible.

Compared to a Web site, a blog is an informal way to display things that are not entirely thought out, or just simple sketches and ideas. The blog format doesn't take itself too seriously, and the work is not really a solid portfolio, it's more of a work in progress. The viewers are free to look at it when they want, but it's up to them. That gives the creator an excuse to post things that are not terribly refined. A Web site portfolio is a real virtual portfolio that should be strong and consistent. A blog is in flux and can't ever be as edited, which is very liberating.

128

If nobody knows about the Web site or blog, you're only doing it for yourself. One part is developing the material and making it available, but the other important part is making it known. Postcard mailers are still an interesting way to draw attention to your online presence. Online stuff always benefits greatly from a presence in the real world. Some artists cross-promote by being active on other blogs (posting comments and links), and by networking in general. Everybody is trying to catch the attention of art directors. It's up to you to make them want check out your work in the first place, and to come back again.

Where to Start

This section is a smattering of references, notes, and pointers for the illustrator who needs to be broadly educated about the Internet.

Illustrators breaking new ground need to understand the importance of learning how to narrow down the options and become more focused in a specific area. This means being patient about the process. Grasping specific details regarding your needs will take time. To quote an old saying, Don't expect a roasted chicken to fly out of the chicken coop. Internet notoriety is not going to be handed to you on a platter. With regard to the marketing of illustration, it is necessary to do your own digging to determine your own special needs, but we can help you begin.

Start with Google. As you may know, in 1998, two Stanford students, Sergey Brin and Larry Page, unveiled their prototype of an Internet search engine that they believed would outperform anything else available at the time. They gave it a quirky name: Google (from the mathematical term "googol" or 10^{100}). Today, Google dominates the search engine business.

Larry Page:

One of the first things we did was just understand the relative importance of things. It used to be in the early days when you did a search for, say, a university, if you did that on an early search engine [such as] Alta Vista, you would get pages that just said 'university' three times in the title. It was based on looking at the text of the documents—that was the traditional way of doing it.

We said, you have all these documents on the Web, why don't we try to figure out in general which ones are more important than others, and then return those? Even in the very early days when we were at Stanford, you could type 'university' into Google, and you actually got the top ten universities. I think that basic notion really helped us a lot. In a sense, it's humans who do the ranking. It's just that we capture everybody's ranking. We looked at things like: How many people link to this page? How do they describe it? What's the text they use in the link itself? You can capture the collective intelligence of all the people who are writing Web pages and use that to help the people who are searching. We use an automated mechanism for capturing all that. It's a sort of group intelligence. That's a powerful idea.

When it comes to marketing your work, using Google to find outlets is invaluable, but making your own decisions based on the data is essential. Group intelligence may aid your quest, but it is no substitute for your own powers of discrimination.

The Importance of the Web Site

Illustrators, for the most part, have Web sites. If you don't have one, make it a priority. Make your Web site more than a slide-show of your work. The Internet is an endless blank page, an opportunity for you to present all the facets of your creations including writing, animation, and story ideas. Add a blog so you have direct contact and communication with the visitors to your site.

Don't make the mistake that many illustrators have made, which is to set up your Web page and forget it. Your Web site is a work in progress, not a stagnant conclusion. You want visitors to return to the site because it is always changing. Included in the Web Directory are Web sites produced by and for a cross-section of illustrators. Check them out. You may find a way of presenting work that you had not thought of.

Questions from an Inquisitive Student

We receive inquiries from students and professionals every week. Some want referrals, others want to understand the key to selling their work. This, to Steven Heller, is one of the more interesting queries with our questionnaire-style answers.

Hi, my name is Robert Decker. I am a senior illustration student at the Rochester Institute of Technology, located in Rochester, New York. One of my assignments before graduating this year is to interview an art director. I was wondering if it would be possible for you to answer a few questions by e-mail when you're free.

Please tell me about your process of specifying image style (photography vs. illustration).

I am no longer an art director per se. I left the *New York Times* as a full-time art director a year ago. Now I consult. My job as I saw it was to expose as many illustrators as possible—good ones, that is—to the world. So my process was to match a good story with a smart artist.

What is your image style preference (photography or illustration), and why?

I much prefer illustration to photography. I think that has to do with my appreciation of handmade imagery dating back to the eighteenth century and the role of satiric art in society at that time through the twentieth century.

Approximately how many illustrations have you used this year?

None, but the year before, approximately three thousand.

Tell me what makes a great illustration portfolio.

One that is well-edited and well-paced, showing an ability to master concept, a range of concepts, good drawing skills, a personality.

What are some of the qualities you expect in an illustrator you would trust to do work for you?

As Woody Allen said, showing up is 80 percent of life. I want an illustrator to be responsible, willing, and enthusiastic, but most of all I want him or her to be smarter than me.

How do you prefer to be contacted by creatives?

I used to meet with artists every morning for five-to-ten-minute interviews. I still believe that one-on-one is the best way to sell oneself.

Is there anything else you might add that will help me begin my career in illustration successfully?

Diversify. The editorial market is not dead, but it is only one of many ways of making and selling mass images.

The Unbearable Burden of Marketing Yourself: A Personal History

The motor that drives the art machine is fueled by energy. Energy is a by product of believing that you have something to say. The fuel for marketing is the desire for money. Desire, in itself, produces craving and depletes energy.

If you desire success you will covet the concept of marketing to fulfill your desires. If you desire communication with yourself and others, that energy base may be the best marketing tool you have.

If all this sounds confusing, it is. Now in my late sixties, after forty years of making pictures that appear on the printed page and gallery wall, I am still confused by Andy Warhol's comment that "The best art of all is the business of art." I am less confused by Mark Rothko's comment, "There is no such thing as a good painting about nothing."

The part of me that paints is not the part of me that markets the painting. Like many artists, I would like to leave the marketing to someone more qualified than myself, but I can't. I wish I could—I have tried. Over the years, I have had a few illustration reps and many gallery owners whose jobs, I thought, were to market me better than I marketed myself. The end result was being forced to acknowledge that I know myself better than they do. Marketing something I believe in is my responsibility. I have tried to make peace with the two parts of me that are in conflict. For example, I set aside specific days to make phone calls, to e-mail, etc. These are the days I don't try and make pictures. This is not a perfect solution, but the tug-of-war between the state of creativity and the state of marketing is less draining.

Looking back is the only way that I can perceive a pattern. If you ask what my next project will be, I will answer, I don't know. If you ask what I have learned about marketing myself over the years, I will answer, I am still learning.

I was educated as a graphic designer (Pratt Institute, 1956–1960). My first job was at General Motors Tech Center. After three months of employment, I realized that I didn't like working with people—I didn't like solving problems that were not my own. The only time I was happy and full of energy was when I was alone, drawing and painting.

My first portfolio was done on 30×40-inch Masoniite boards and weighed sixty pounds. A marketing expert would have talked me out of it. Many art directors stopped me on Madison Avenue and asked what was in the portfolio-on-wheels. The card I gave out was an original painting of a man playing a paintbrush with a violin bow. A marketing expert would have sent me to a printer. The card sat, framed, on many art directors' desks. The card included my name, address, and phone number, but the phone, unfortunately, was located at my friend's house a half-block away from my apartment in Brooklyn. The art director who called me for my first illustration job was put on hold for the ten minutes it took my friend to run down the block and get me. The art director, thinking I had listed the candy store on the corner, told me to never get my own phone.

"Meaning," Carl Jung said, "has curative power. What is meaningful to you is the basis of all things, perhaps everything."

My advice is simply to accept the responsibility of marketing yourself. If you are marketing for yourself, it will provide you with the energy to do it all.

A kung-fu master told me this about replenishing energy: hug trees. My advice: make more art.

—Marshall Arisman

Chapter Seven

Working in Traditional and New Media

Illustrators are increasingly adapting to the fact that their creative juices will be needed in a wide array of new communications industries. The traditional may be popular this year (and next) but in a few more, that will change. As print migrates to the Web (and other digital platforms), illustrators will merge with designers to create visual content. While few of our respondents would call themselves "mergers," most agree that the new technologies are their new reality. What's more, those who responded positively to branching out agree that image making is definitely not confined to editorial, although they all agree that print is not dead.

Bob Staake: Damn Lazy!

What are the three most recent jobs you've done?

An illo for MAD *magazine, a cover for the* Wall Street Journal, *and a feature illo for the* Washington Post. *Yesterday it was two illos for* Barron's *and at the same time I was inserting maybe eight pencil sketches for* New Yorker *covers. At the same time, I'm working on a new pop-up children's picture book and finishing a 5 × 3-foot poster that will be used by the publisher to shill the book.*

Which of these jobs were done for a venue or medium that was untraditional (not editorial)?

If you consider children's picture books within or outside of traditional 'editorial,' the answer will change. I do about three to five children's books a year now, and with multi-book deals from Random House, Simon and Schuster, Little, Brown, etc. that is accounting for maybe 50 percent of my annual income. Personally, I definitely consider books non-editorial—especially because they straddle image and text (writing and illustrating my titles) and push into toys and novelty (pop-up books). I also do so much weird stuff that is so far out of the realm of my usual stuff that I almost never tell anybody about it. For example, I just licensed a book/novelty to Cider Mill Press last week [that enables] people to grow their own desktop crop circle from grass seeds and templates. I'm in the middle of developing two games for a client I can't name—one (Flast) dubbed 'the most beautiful word game ever' by a Washington Post *focus group, and a 'parlor' game (man, I hate that term) that can best be described as a cross between charades and truth-or-dare [that consists] of nothing more than three thousand cards written and designed by me and served up in a small, multi-colored box. It is called the I Game.*

How much of your work is done for traditional (i.e., print) and untraditional (i.e., digital, toys, textiles, murals) media?

Truly varies from month to month. This year maybe 50 percent.

What is the most challenging untraditional medium you've worked in?

I thought doing pop-up books was going to be insane, and it simply has not played out that way. I am on my second pop-up for Little, Brown. From the very beginning of these books, I need to establish a solid mental picture of what I want taking place in the book and then my flat, 2-D pencil sketches need to suggest that action (elements rising, elements coming forward, elements moving when opened, etc). The paper engineers in Asia then take it to the next level and create a prototype, and 50 percent of the time they are dead-on, but other times I will have to take the proto and tweak—usually to get more drama and 'believability' in a scene (as if a hippo flying a bi-plane is ever believable). This weekend I'm designing a surfboard—I think this is my fourth. They're always fun—but then they get all waxed and dinged up.

Surfboard designed by Bob Staake.

Who are your primary clients?

The New Yorker, *the* Washington Post, MAD *magazine, the* Wall Street Journal, Barron's, *the* Christian Science Monitor, *Random House, Simon and Schuster, Little, Brown, Viking, and a bunch of others that I'm probably forgetting.*

What new technologies have you had to master?

I'm so damn lazy. I started working digitally in 1995 in Adobe Photoshop 3.0, and that's still the only thing I work in (Photoshop 3.0—not CS 3).

How has your illustration changed to meet the new technologies?

I used to be known as the guy who did all these crazy, cartoonish crowd scenes in kids' magazines, on cereal boxes, on products, etc. When I started working digitally I was concerned that my style would change—and that would have been a stupid thing to [have had] occur because I was very successful and making a comfortable living as a humorous illustrator. Still, I have always been a huge, huge fan of modernism, and in particular, mid-century European poster art (Cassandre, Carlu, Morvan, Brun, Leupin, Steinweiss, et al.). In 1997, I stumbled upon a way to get a Photoshop brush to 'spatter' and appear like the toothbrush effects that many of the great poster artists used to achieve shading, cast shadows, accentuation, etc. I came up with this idea for an ABC board book for Simon and Schuster. As more and more clients saw this 'new' approach of mine, they wanted to use [my new work] rather than my traditional stuff, and I was feeling the same way: losing interest in cartooning and wanting to express my more 'sophisticated,' design-oriented side. I decided to split myself in two, offering clients the opportunity to have me work in 'normal Bob' (pen and ink colored in Photoshop) or 'digital Bob' (100 percent Photoshop). At first it was 50/50, but soon it became 80-percent-digital Bob/20-percent-normal Bob. Don't get me wrong, I love to draw (I still continue to do a weekly drawing for the the Washington Post—something I have done every week for fifteen years), but there's something about pugging, tugging, and yanking on a mouse to create an image that I just love. It's a little like drawing with a bar of soap, but somehow it works for me. Go figure!

Christoph Abbrederis: Cardboard, Ink, or Gouache

What are the three most recent jobs you've done?

1. *Illustrations for the German newspaper* Sueddeutsche Zeitung
2. Moritaten, *an illustrated book based on sinister songs/lyrics on real murder cases from the beginning of the twentieth century*
3. Football Heroes, *portraits of the German soccer team of 1976*

Which of these jobs were done for a venue or medium that was untraditional (not editorial)?

Images from Football Heroes *were also presented on a Web site.*

How much of your work is done for traditional (i.e., print) and untraditional (i.e., digital, toys, textiles, murals) media?

Most of my work is done in a traditional manner: on cardboard with ink and/ or gouache [paints]. Some of my illustrations were used in an untraditional way, as in advertising. [For example,] I created a logo for a Swiss cloth company, Blue Dog. The blue dog was also produced as a mascot, a toy, a candle, and a label for beer bottles. It also got animated for TV and cinema.

I designed a fictive City for SMART/Mercedes, which was used as a virtual reality video in order to show the benefits of the new product.

[I've done] textile and glass design.

I designed an interactive Web site for a brewing company based on illustrated characters.

What is the most challenging untraditional medium you've worked in?

Animation of my drawings.

Who are your primary clients?

Publishing houses, magazines, and newspapers.

What new technologies have you had to master?

Photoshop, InDesign, and Illustrator.

How has your illustration changed to meet the new technologies?

I started to use the possibilities of the new technologies to change or enrich my images in the early '90s. Later on I returned to a more traditional way in my illustration work and [began to] use computer programs mostly to make corrections, digitize, transport, and archive my images. However, I now see computer-based sketching and design as an essential part of modern illustration, and both traditional- and computer-based techniques can complement each other successfully.

Christoph Abbrederis's Blue Dog.

Edel Rodriguez: Back and Forth

What are the three most recent jobs you've done?

1. *Back page essay illustration for* Time *magazine*
2. *Illustration of Shakespeare's* As You Like It *for Soulpepper Theater in Canada*
3. *Illustration of South by Southwest festival for* Billboard *magazine*

SOULPEPPER THEATRE 10TH ANNIVERSARY SEASON FEB 27 – APR 19

08 **AS YOU LIKE IT**
WILLIAM SHAKESPEARE

As You Like It poster designed by Edel Rodriguez.

Which of these jobs were done for a venue or media that was untraditional (not editorial)?

The image for As You Like It *was used on posters around the city, on the theater's Web site, [on] collateral material, etc.*

How much of your work is done for traditional (i.e., print) and untraditional (i.e., digital, toys, textiles, murals) media?

I'd say it's probably 80 percent traditional and 20 percent untraditional, but there is a lot of overlap. Many times, clients want to use [an] image for print and then create some other digital use. I see both print and digital working together quite a bit.

What is the most challenging untraditional medium you've worked in?

Animation. It's a whole other way of thinking, more about timing than [about] the details and textures of a static image.

Who are your primary clients?

The New Yorker, Time *magazine,* Playboy, *Random House, Little, Brown (publishes my kids' books).*

What new technologies have you had to master?

I'm working on learning more about Web design so I can put together sites for my various projects. I haven't mastered the technology, though. Far from it!

How has your illustration changed to meet the new technologies?

My work hasn't changed to meet a particular technology. I've used the technology to express some of my visual ideas. My output now is about 50 percent traditional and 50 percent [of a] mix [between] digital and traditional. I enjoy going back and forth between the two, but haven't felt I had to do this to meet a particular need.

Felix Sockwell: Sculptures From Wire

What are the most recent jobs you've done?

Today I finished out a library (twenty [images]) for US Cellular. I'm also working on a series of prints for the Burlington [Sound of Music] Festival, as well as a new identity for Public Citizen.

"Butch's Brain" by Felix Sockwell.

Which of these jobs were done for a venue or medium that was untraditional (not editorial)?

None were editorial. Most of my work is advertising, corporate, and iconography.

How much of your work is done for traditional (i.e., print) and untraditional (i.e., digital, toys, textiles, murals) media?

My guesstimate: 40 percent advertising, corporate; 30 percent editorial (print); 20 percent logos, animations, and icons; 10 percent pro bono/political/personal/ donations.

What is the most challenging untraditional medium you've worked in?

Making sculptures from wire, string, ribbon, and other materials. Also, doing portraits of kids in the park was a total nightmare.

Who are your primary clients?

This year: Herman Miller (that was half my salary), Sony, American Express, Hotels.com, and, of course, my favorite client is the New York Times.

What new technologies have you had to master?

E-mail and bullshitting.

How has your illustration changed to meet the new technologies?

I bought a Wacom Cintiq that allows me to never actually draw on paper. I whip everything out right on the screen. 'Butch's Brain' is a fine example (he owns the wine bar in Zeeland, Michigan, where most of Herman Miller's employees unwind). Christoph Niemann and I bought our Cintiqs at ICON in San Francisco a few years ago, but he is much, much faster on it [than I am]. He's actually a robot.

Gary Taxali: E-mail-Challenged

What are the three most recent jobs you've done?

1. *Album cover art and inside art package for Aimee Mann*
2. *Poster for Thinktopia*
3. *Full-page illustration for Wallspace*

Which of these jobs were done for a venue or medium that was untraditional (not editorial)?

Two were untraditional, one was editorial.

Gary Taxali illustrations.

How much of your work is done for traditional (i.e., print) and untraditional (i.e., digital, toys, textiles, murals) media?

30 percent traditional. 70 percent toys, fine art, etc.

What is the most challenging untraditional medium you've worked in?

Creating forty-plus wine labels for Bonny Doon vineyard. [It was] challenging in the sense that I always tried to do something different.

Who are your primary clients?

These days, it's all over the place and things happen in phases with different clients.

What new technologies have you had to master?

Opening attachments in Webmail.

How has your illustration changed to meet the new technologies?

If it has, I am unaware of how.

Gilbert Ford: Man of Layers

What are the three most recent jobs you've done?

1. Johns Hopkins *magazine essay spot*
2. *Little, Brown Books for Young Readers cover and interior chapter illustrations for a middle-grade chapter book*
3. *Currently working on five spots for* Teen *magazine*

Which of these jobs were done for a venue or medium that was untraditional (not editorial)?

Little, Brown is pretty untraditional. It's not so much the actual process of illustrating the book but the assignments that derive from them in regards to promotion. For the chapter book series, they wanted me to illustrate an amusement park that would be animated [and posted] online to promote the books. I also had to create downloadable, printer-friendly 'prizes' that could be cut and assembled into 3-D circus animals. So there was a lot of experimentation with cutting, bending, and folding paper before [I started] making the illustration.

How much of your work is done for traditional (i.e., print) and untraditional (i.e., digital, toys, textiles, murals) media?

I would say about 30 percent is untraditional these days.

What is the most challenging untraditional medium you've worked in?

I made 3-D puzzles for Mudpuppy/Galison. It was challenging to create the template and make sure each 3-D toy could stand when assembled. I had to find the balance between making the toy both fun [and] educational, and then create the packaging to reflect that.

Who are your primary clients?

They change a lot, but the book publishing clients seem to be the most loyal.

What new technologies have you had to master?

I don't know if I have mastered any of them, but I have a general understanding of Photoshop, Illustrator, Flash, Dreamweaver, GarageBand, Quark, InDesign, etc., and I have used all of them to sell ideas or get work.

Mudpuppy/Galison 3-D puzzles designed by Gilbert Ford.

147

How has your illustration changed to meet the new technologies?

Everything has to be in layers because people expect you to make changes up until the last minute, so my work has changed from being an actual painting to existing only on the screen.

Hannoch Piven: Junk Man

What are the three most recent jobs you've done?

I just finished a caricature of Mahmoud Ahmadinejad for a bi-weekly column I have in the weekend supplement of the Israeli newspapaer Maariv, *an illustration about wedding registries for* Modern Bride *magazine, and a TV program for Catalonian TV where my hands are filmed creating with objects and with some stop-motion animation.*

Which of these jobs were done for a venue or medium that was untraditional (not editorial)?

[The first two were] traditional; [the third,] untraditional.

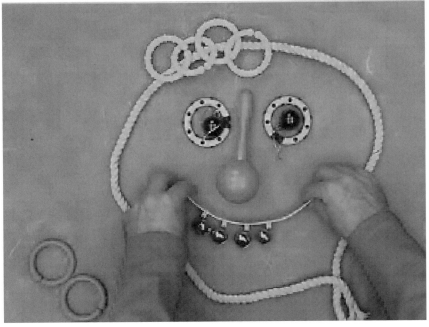

Hannoch Piven creates a stop-motion animation.

How much of your work is done for traditional (i.e., print) and untraditional (i.e., digital, toys, textiles, murals, etc.) media?

I'd say 60 to 70 percent of my work is still editorial of some sort or another, though in the last year I have gotten involved in these two TV programs, which are now taking much of my time.

What is the most challenging untraditional medium you've worked in?

Doing sculptures with garbage found in a junkyard and placing them in the City Hall of the town where the junkyard is.

Who are your primary clients?

[It] really changes by the year. Right now Maariv *(a newspaper from Israel TV3), Catalonian public TV, and* AARP *magazine in D.C., where I have a regular gig.*

What new technologies have you had to master?

I am not a heavy Photoshop user, though I do use it on every piece. I don't really use new technologies, but every now and then I do large sculptures, and for that I need to deal with issues of welding, screwing, gluing, maintenance, warranties—things that, as an illustrator, I never had to deal with. So for that I usually get a helper; I still don't weld.

How has your illustration changed to meet the new technologies?

[It hasn't] exactly. But in some cases, like in sculptures, perishable items are not to be used.

Isabelle Dervaux: Small Buttons

What are the three most recent jobs you've done?

Lately, I have been getting a lot of assignments about stress reduction, just feeling good in your body and changing your life. First was a small spot for Pilates *magazine; second, a series of illustrations for a press kit for the French company Tena, which focuses on incontinence products for women—they needed to revamp their image and they asked me to help them shed their old image! [I'd] never done anything like that. Third, I just finished the cover of the weekend section for the* Washington Post. *I was busy with the preparation of the ICON5 Conference in New York, so I was happy when the art director, Marty Barrick, told me they had a concept already. Marty was apologetic about it; I thought, Good! No searching around for a clever concept, things will move faster. Usually I would want to come up with the concept, which is the best part of the job. I just had to make the composition work with their layout. It involved handwritten lettering, which I enjoy doing.*

Which of these jobs were done for a venue or medium that was untraditional (not editorial)?

Not very recently, but last year, I had a fun assignment doing interactive illustrations for [the Web site of] a Japanese company, Sekisui House, which is an Osaka firm [that] manufactures and customizes houses and designs landscapes. I had to draw a cutout of a single-family house, along with a series of characters that would live in it. They moved from room to room, and established a whole dialogue with the user. The studio animated the whole thing in Flash; I just did the key frames for the characters' movements. Earlier on in my career, I did some surface design, [did] some T-shirt designs, designed an inflatable plastic doll for a point of purchase display, and came up with the concept of a department store window.

How much of your work is done for traditional (i.e., print) and untraditional (i.e., digital, toys, textiles) media?

I get a lot of calls for illustration for Web sites. There is an increasing market for small icons/buttons to organize information. Studios or ad agencies approach me with ambitious ideas—unfortunately, often these types of calls don't pan out because clients do not have the budget for them. I have had many experiences where clients thought they could wing it by putting some illustrations on their homepage to get a look and feel for the whole Web site. They think that they can brand their whole identity with a few stock illustrations and add a few new ones here and there. They feel that they can get away [with] not paying much because they are a start-up or whatever. I generalize, but art buyers don't want to pay much for anything commissioned for the Web. You have to fight a lot to get the right price for the use. Small businesses need to be educated in using illustration on Web sites [because] they don't see it as an investment for their brand.

What is the most challenging untraditional medium you've worked in?

I had to do a mural once for a Barneys New York showroom, where I had to work directly with paint on the wall—which I never do—and work everything very fast, which was a challenge for me.

Isabelle Dervaux illustrations.

Who are your primary clients?

I have been working regularly with the artisanal bakery Bay Bread here in San Francisco. I have done promotional cards and a T-shirt. Plans to sell cards in their store, use illustrations on their Web site, and create kids' menus and other material for their stores are in the works.

What new technologies have you had to master?

I use Illustrator and Photoshop. I use the basic functions; I haven't explored the whole spectrum of tools in [them]. [I] need to learn a few more things at each update. Basically, I use [them] for coloring and scaling. I scan my black-and-white brush line. I used to do everything black-and-white and specify color or cut Pantone films for getting nice flat colors, adding a black overlay on top. It is fantastic to be able to try out background colors so easily with Illustrator, although I usually agonize in trying to decide which CMYK percentages to use. My husband took a class in Flash; seeing him [go] through [it] made me realize it was not [for] me.

How has your illustration changed to meet the new technologies?

[It hasn't] really. I adapted, and I gained a lot of flexibility. One problem that is happening now is that an illustration is never really finished; I feel that I always want to correct something when I open my files and see the illustration with a fresh eye, even if the illustration has been sent off. I want to move an element one pixel left or right or fix the line that has been vectorized. The number of versions I have of the same illustration can get ridiculous.

Leonetto Calvetti: 3-D Digital

What are the three most recent jobs you've done?

1. Point-of-sale illustration for Planters (Kraft)
2. Packaging illustration for Refresh Eye Tears
3. Casino craps table for online gaming

Which of these jobs were done for a venue or medium that was untraditional (not editorial)?

I would say only the online casino job. But if we mean untraditional technique, all my works are made by the 3-D digital technique, which is not yet a traditional one.

How much of your work is done for traditional (i.e., print) and untraditional (i.e., digital, toys, textiles, murals) media?

I would say that 70 percent of my work it is still for traditional print.

What is the most challenging untraditional medium you've worked in?

Well, in my case, animation is the most challenging medium—probably because I started working on it not too long ago—and hopefully soon it will become easier.

Who are your primary clients?

Advertising agencies for packaging and printed campaigns, and publishers for nonfiction children's books.

What new technologies have you had to master?

The 3-D digital modeling and rendering is a never-ending, developing technology. You need to stay up-to-date constantly, learning new software versions, plug-ins, and brand-new softwares continuously.

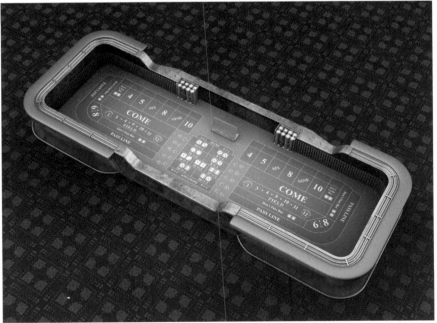

Online craps table created by Leonetto Calvetti.

How has your illustration changed to meet the new technologies?

If you consider that, until 1999, I was still working [with] airbrush and brushes, my illustration [has] changed very much in terms of media. But my style didn't change so much, because this was what I wanted.

Lou Brooks: The Fine Art World

What are the three most recent jobs you've done?

A lot of my projects these days are self-generated, such as illustrated books and fine art, but I assume you mean illustration jobs assigned by commercial art buyers, so here are the latest three:

1. Time *magazine cover: annual mind & body special issue*
2. Texas Monthly *inside half-page about how to finance a border wall between the United States and Mexico*
3. Sound & Vision *magazine full-page feature opener about phonograph turntables*
   All three are pen-and-ink on watercolor paper along with subsequent Photoshop techniques.

The Texas Monthly *'wall' piece is an example of editors allowing me to take the assignment beyond just an illustration image; being allowed to conceive, write, and illustrate the space. It's something I can do well.*

The Sound & Vision *piece is an example of the editors trusting me to transform a dry-tech assignment into something that stops the readers in their tracks. In this case, they allowed me to trash their original headline and replace it with something more fun.*

Which of these jobs were done for a venue or media that was untraditional (not editorial)?

All three of the above jobs were traditional editorial assignments for magazine publishers. Most illustrators that I know seem to concentrate on editorial. To me, magazine and book assignments are usually more interesting than advertising work, even though publishing has strangely become a realm ruled by editors. There are still some really great editorial [art directors] in the business, but some seem to have checked their balls at the door when they took the job, and I don't mean 'balls' here as any sort of gender observation. At some publishing offices, I think there's what's known as a 'ball room' somewhere. It's where the cloakroom used to be.

I don't pursue advertising assignments like I used to, which can be an expensive attitude to have. [Advertising] can be an evil business that makes a lot of money to convince us to do things we shouldn't do. People say that television exists because of advertising, but it's the other way around. Advertising exists because of television. And a lot of the hotshots out of design school tend toward what they feel will be the excitement of broadcast. I suppose many are dreaming of that TV-commercial-to-film-director leap. That's not to say I don't still consider an ad project whenever one comes along. It depends on the integrity of the project—and, oh yeah, if they've got a bajillion dollars. Then I tell them to hold on while I go get Mr. Brooks on the phone for them. What the hell do I care whether somebody smokes or not?

How much of your work is done for traditional (i.e., print) and untraditional (i.e., digital, toys, textiles, murals) media?

I'm not sure I categorically fit so neatly into some of these questions. A good chunk of my revenue now comes from my own stock illustration library, which has grown to the point where I now carefully manage it through a stock agency that I'm really happy with. It's licensed for all sorts of media. Around fifteen years ago, I was one of the first to consider re-selling existing art, I think. After a long illustration career, it's the only tangible equity we have. If done right—which, among other things, means keeping re-use fees up with original assignment fees—I see it as a viable means of survival in a much-eroded industry, as well as a way to free up your time, which means more options.

Traditional print illustration has its place in my world, at least for now. A bit of the other venues you mention are starting to appear for me. I'd like to do some 'artist' toys, but I haven't really gone after that yet. And we all have enough of those little green and purple rubber alien toys with the scary teeth in them, don't we?

What is the most challenging untraditional medium you've worked in?

Lately, I would say that the fine art world is the most challenging. Paint on canvas has its limitations. And it's hard work; you have to stand up a lot. I've quickly found fine art to be probably the most crassly commercial area of art I've ever encountered. And I've heard that's where the [phrase] 'there's no accounting for taste' was first used. I hope I'm not getting the hairy eyeball from the gallery world as I'm saying all this, because I need the money! But it's mostly in the marketing, I think, rather than the art.

Who are your primary clients?

For the last five years, as far as assignments, I've focused my attention primarily on editorial clients, which means mostly magazines and book publishers.

What new technologies have you had to master?

I take to digital thinking pretty easily, and I have no problem taking on a new software if it gets me to where I want to go. Or even better, [if] it surprises me. The trick is to think like your Mac thinks—it sure ain't gonna do the same for you.

Adobe Flash especially is a program whose logic process lies somewhere within Superman's Bizarro World. I'm trying to get the hang of the latest CS3 version. It's formidable, making Flash movies that aren't crap—which is what most online Flash movies are. You can lose years of your life in there if you're not careful. But moving your art and things like sound and time around—it can take your breath away.

How has your illustration changed to meet the new technologies?

The answer to this one requires a (hopefully) concise history. I've never been able to get rid of this harmful obsession [with] inking a line as perfectly as it can be inked. It's the only way I'm satisfied. [It's] something my parents did to me. And let me tell you, inking on Mylar with a #00 Rapidograph and Alvin French curves, then shaving each point and corner with a #16 X–Acto until five in the morning can be bad for the liver. My wife says it's like watching a man polish a car, and he can't stop. I called it a 'harmful obsession' because, from the start, the whole deal just slowed me down to a crawl while the phone kept ringing with more and more assignments. Madness.

It lasted up until the early '90s, when I plugged in my first Mac Centris and realized that it and Adobe Illustrator could make a really, really perfect line a lot faster. The greatest thing since sliced beer.

So, to give you half the answer to your question: My working process changed dramatically to 'meet the new technologies,' but it was my intention that the look of my art stay exactly the same, which it did. Way back then, I was obsessing on the 'brand' aspect of my art. I loved that I was using all of this sophisticated tech and that people weren't really much aware of it. I still feel that way about my digital art. It's a magic trick. However, I eventually learned that the problem with making a perfect line in Illustrator is that every Joe Schmoe can do it, and has.

That brings us to the second half of my answer: my illustration has changed over the last five years to meet the old technologies. I've discovered the pencil, pen, and paper. The pencil's got this little red rubber 'delete' thing on the other end called an "eraser." Really cool. Around five years ago, if you paid attention, you picked up this vibe that people were not so much getting fed up with computers, but rather were getting fed up with the perfection that it was creating. People were needing to reconnect with themselves in a tactile way. So, I draw with pencil and pen on paper. Then I give the drawing to our cats to play with, then I back

156

our pick-up truck over it, and so on. It's never the same twice. But eventually, it goes back into the Mac where I mix it up in there with some other tricks until it simulates tactile imperfection perfectly.

Speaking for myself, the future in illustration lies in being able to do many things. The days of illustrators sitting around until the phone rang obviously

Lou Brooks *Time* magazine cover.

ain't happening much anymore, is it? There are still specialists among us, but most of them work very fast, or have really rich parents. An atmosphere of desperate creativity now exists, which is great, because you get convinced that anything can happen. For me, I see now that it's never going to end. There are too many options. So hooray for all [of] it!

Neil Numberman: Slightly Untraditional

What are the three most recent jobs you've done?

I'm currently working on two graphic novels for kids published by Henry Holt Books for Young Readers about a fly who is also a private eye, and a picture book for Greenwillow Books about a boy who regrets building his own Frankenstein [monster].

And the most recent before that was a few cartoons for Radar *magazine (online) to accompany an article on the entertainment value of a visit to the Scientology Headquarters.*

Which of these jobs were done for a venue or medium that was untraditional (not editorial)?

Each one is slightly untraditional in its own way. The picture book [is untraditional] because I'm bringing many characteristics of comic books to the picture book medium, including the use of word balloons, panels, and 'sound words' (like CRASH! BANG! GASP!).

The Joey Fly: Private Eye *books are only untraditional in the sense that they are bringing the graphic novel, as opposed to the comic book, to a much younger audience (eight or nine years old), which seems like a fairly new concept that's only started taking off in the last couple years.*

The Scientology article was Web-only, which is completely untraditional compared with ten years ago or so. It was also unique in the way that I was hired to do the piece: Radar *commissioned a comedy-writer friend of mine and myself to 'infiltrate' the Scientology Headquarters by spending a day there, getting tours, watching their films, and being evaluated by them. Untraditional...and scary.*

How much of your work is done for traditional (i.e., print) and untraditional (i.e., digital, toys, textiles, murals) media?

I'd say most of the work I do is for print. Sometimes, even if it's not originally for print, a piece will still find its way to the presses. It seems that people still want a hard copy these days. Let's hope that continues.

What is the most challenging untraditional medium you've worked in?

I used to do a lot of animation on the old pencil test machines, and it worked very well with the way that I think. When I first started experimenting with Flash, some of the ways they went about shortcutting were completely foreign and rather annoying to me. As far as animation goes, I still just can't completely wrap my

Illustration by Neil Numberman.

head around Flash, although I've been happy with one or two cartoons I've done in it. Adobe ImageReady is much more up my alley, and definitely takes the old pencil test approach to animating.

Who are your primary clients?

Children's book publishers.

What new technologies have you had to master?

They're not quite 'new' exactly, but as a former technophobe, Photoshop, HTML, and Flash were, and are, quite a pain to learn.

How has your illustration changed to meet the new technologies?

Before I started scanning my work into Photoshop, I had a lot of trouble working in the traditional media, like paint, etching, screen printing, and even ink. Mistakes are easily corrected when the computer's got your back, and lord knows I'm full of them.

Nick Craine: More Spontaneous

What are the three most recent jobs you've done?

1. 'The Power Paradox' for the UTNE Reader *(art director – Stephanie Glaros)*
2. A series of spot illos for the Walrus *(art director – Anthony E. DeLuca)*
3. Smirnoff Vodka concept illos for Launch! Brand Marketing (creative director – Liesbeth Lenard)

Which of these jobs were done for a venue or medium that was untraditional (not editorial)?

The Smirnoff Vodka concept illos (electronic pieces are used as sales tools for product launches between sales teams, i.e., marketing and end client).

How much of your work is done for traditional (i.e., print) and untraditional (i.e., digital, toys, textiles, murals) media?

65 percent.

What is the most challenging untraditional medium you've worked in?

A series of museum panels for The Charlton Martello Tower Museum, Charlton, Saint John, Canada. The client needed me to visualize the construction of a

Nick Craine illustration.

Martello Tower, though no guide to creating one exists. The structure of the thing leaves no conclusive evidence as to how the builders would have created the 360-degree arc. I was having to hypothesize the construction process based on photos. It was challenging because the piece serves as a historical document and therefore had to be as authentic as possible.

Who are your primary clients?

Magazines and newspapers.

What new technologies have you had to master?

The Wacom tablet, Photoshop.

How has your illustration changed to meet the new technologies?

The technology has become a teaching tool for me and has made my illustration much more expressive and spontaneous. The 'undo' function has given me a safety net. Before the computer, I was tentative with color and line (afraid to commit), but now experimentation has become consequence-free. It no longer becomes about a specific color. Instead it's about color relationships. The idea trumps [the] execution. I like the monkish notion that people ought to learn to paint light, to endure the education, but I think, as a species, we've grown accustomed to filling in the implied notes. Now the person who constructs images can cut straight to the structure of the thing and not worry too much about sheen. The pieces are more spatial value equations and less decorative. This evolution in technology is bringing the wire frame into the center.

The machine lets me distress the work, to change the temperature of a piece, to merge multiple versions of an image together, etc. When I bring my drawing into Photoshop, the process is a lot more like sculpture and figuring out when to stop fussing with it. Illustration becomes much more of a conversation between myself and the work. The machine provides this wonderful bath to fix the image in. It's exciting because I don't always know what will happen, and as a result, it's teaching me to always be open, to see the narrative associations as they present themselves. This sort of freedom has made me rediscover the pencil. Now I draw with a ferocious speed and enjoy revising the sketch many times.

Peter Blegvad: Dither and Procrastinate

What are the three most recent jobs you've done?

1. *Cover for* The Grindstone of Rapport, a Clayton Eshleman Reader *to be published by Black Widow Press in Boston*
2. *'State of the Art,' a monthly cartoon I've been doing for [about] two years for the* Word, *a music (and more!) magazine based in London*
3. *Contributing art to [a] Web site promoting BBC Radio 3's Free Thinking Festival*

Which of these jobs were done for a venue or medium that was untraditional (not editorial)?

I don't think any of these were traditionally editorial.

How much of your work is done for traditional (i.e., print) and untraditional (i.e., digital, toys, textiles, murals) media?

The BBC Web site was a rare foray into such untraditional media for me; though the technical assembly was all done by a design team, I just contributed the images and sounds.

162

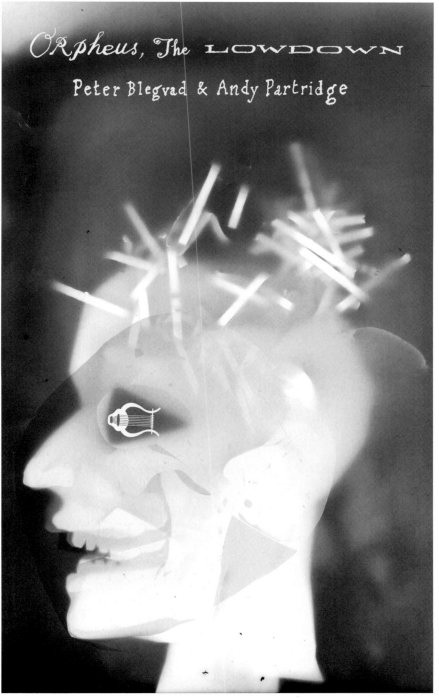

Orpheus, The LOWDOWN

Peter Blegvad & Andy Partridge

What is the most challenging untraditional medium you've worked in?

The DVD I made for De Balie (center for culture and politics in Amsterdam), which was published with The Book of Imaginary Media.

The DVD is a recording of a performance/lecture on the subject with songs and about eighty illustrations. De Balie's technical team put [together] the materials I supplied.

Who are your primary clients?

Magazines, occasional publishers, [and] record companies.

What new technologies have you had to master?

Photoshop, iMovie.

How has your illustration changed to meet the new technologies?

For better or worse, Photoshop allows one to dither and procrastinate, to delay commitment—I guess that's for worse. But the concomitant upside is the carte blanche to try radical transformations without destroying an original.

I like using layers in Photoshop; it reminds me of printmaking at art school, which I loved. Not the same, of course—unphysical/immaterial—but a lot easier for those of us without a press, and pretty damn cool in its own right.

Peter Sis: Simpler and Bolder

What are the three most recent jobs you've done?

1. *The children's playroom in a new building going up at 200 West End Avenue [in New York]*
2. *A cover for a book being put together by Amnesty International to celebrate the Declaration of Human Rights*
3. *A painting done on a washboard*

Which of these jobs were done for a venue or media that was untraditional (not editorial)?

All of the above.

A children's playroom designed by Peter Sis.

How much of your work is done for traditional (i.e., print) and untraditional (i.e., digital, toys, textiles, murals) media?

80/20, but it is changing toward untraditional.

What is the most challenging untraditional medium you've worked in?

I painted a skateboard once.

Who are your primary clients?

Book publishers.

What new technologies have you had to master?

A large-scale mosaic.

How has your illustration changed to meet the new technologies?

My work has become simpler and bolder.

Ray Bartkus: Digital Video

What are the three most recent jobs you've done?

1. A cover for Harper's magazine
2. A cover for the Wall Street Journal Weekend Edition
3. An installation for DIVA NY '08 (digital and video art fair)

Which of these jobs were done for a venue or medium that was untraditional (not editorial)?

Diva NY '08: I had to create an installation out of my digital prints. I exhibited these prints as transparencies in light boxes.

How much of your work is done for traditional (i.e., print) and untraditional (i.e., digital, toys, textiles, murals) media?

I think the 'untraditional' portion is getting exponentially larger with every passing year.

What is the most challenging untraditional medium you've worked in?

Digital video; there are many components to master: movement, sequencing, audio, lighting, and editing.

Who are your primary clients?

Myself, the Wall Street Journal, Advertisement Age, *[and the] Vartai Gallery.*

What new technologies have you had to master?

While working on the piece 'One Man and 300 Million People,' I had to learn how to direct the actors and how to produce work outside the walls of my

Still from Bartkus' "One Man and 300 Million People."

studio, while passersby were giggling and distracting me with their comments. I learned a lot of stuff that has more to do with film-making than illustrating.

How has your illustration changed to meet the new technologies?

For me, the starting point to creating an illustration—or piece of artwork in general—is always an idea, the concept I want to explore using visual means. When the idea crystallizes in my head, I choose the technologies I think will suit the representation of that particular idea the best; therefore, I don't think that the technologies themselves are the driving force behind the change in my illustration style. Technological advances, however, change the way I experience the world and this consequently changes the ideas on which my works are based.

Richard Turtletaub: Dreamlike Imagery

What are the three most recent jobs you've done?

1. *Illustrations for* Newsweek International Edition *(subject: globalization)*
2. *The 50th Grammy Awards program book (section opening page illo on the Grammy organization)*
3. *Motion graphics dream sequence for Kelly Ebsary's 'What's Eating Kate?,' a live multimedia performance as part of the REDCAT studio in Los Angeles*

Which of these jobs were done for a venue or media that was untraditional (not editorial)?

In Kelly Ebsary's 'What's Eating Kate?,' I put together a motion graphics sequence [that] was projected behind a single actor on stage as part of a live multimedia performance. This sequence, which used old photos of Kate Smith incorporated in dreamlike imagery made up of land, skyscapes, musical notation, and floating TV sets, culminated with the actor 'conversing' with Kate Smith (or a projected montage of a Kate Smith portrait and the actor's mouth).

How much of your work is done for traditional (i.e., print) and untraditional (i.e., digital, toys, textiles, murals) media?

Currently about half traditional, half untraditional.

What is the most challenging untraditional medium you've worked in?

Definitely motion graphics. It is the most challenging in terms of learning the software, but also the most rewarding.

Who are your primary clients?

The New York Times, *the* San Francisco Chronicle, *and various SourceMedia publications.*

What new technologies have you had to master?

Motion graphics software, [i.e.,] Adobe After Effects. [I'm also] learning Cinema 4D.

How has your illustration changed to meet the new technologies?

Around 1990, back in what feels to me like the Stone Age, I began illustrating using color Xerox-cutout images with the occasional airbrush. By the mid-'90s I was using Adobe Photoshop, which made the process much easier and allowed me many more options, such as working with transparency and more extreme manipulation of color. It also resulted in cleaner, neater edges and smoother gradations in the work—especially since I never quite mastered the airbrush.

Image created by Richard Turtletaub.

In the last few years, I began using Adobe After Effects to do motion graphics. The style that I gravitate [toward] is fairly fast-paced and imagery-intensive. My effort in coming up with the necessary imagery has resulted in my reaching in lots of directions that were new to me, such as the use of video footage, lighting effects, and 3-D effects, and the interplay of transparency modes, all for a project that might be thirty seconds long. This has certainly spilled over into the way I think about illustration assignments. Now I'm more likely to try out some different looks than I would have [been] when I had to cut and paste.

Simon Spilsbury: Nappies on the Web

What are the three most recent jobs you've done?

[Jobs for] Cobra beer, Huggies nappies, [and the] London Electoral Commission.

Which of these jobs were done for a venue or medium that was untraditional (not editorial)?

Cobra — TV, print, Web; Huggies — TV, print, Web; London Elect — print, Web

How much of your work is done for traditional (i.e., print) and untraditional (i.e., digital, toys, textiles, murals) media?

Most is still traditional, albeit the majority of clients now buy usage for Web applications, including phone, and other alternative media are increasingly creeping in. Live art is also becoming more popular (i.e., murals, shop windows, etc.).

What is the most challenging untraditional medium you've worked in?

Designing a toy in Cinema 4D was a departure from my normal work. [The] most challenging aspect was aligning the drawing to the model.

Who are your primary clients?

Ad agencies.

What new technologies have you had to master?

From a creative directing point of view—not an operating one—I've had to familiarize myself with various software, including Cinema 4D. To maximize my output as an illustrator in new media, I set up 'artbombers' with an

Simon Spilsbury illustration.

illustrator who works exclusively digitally. This way we still get to be good at what we're good at individually, but mix the two disciplines to create a third artist.

How has your illustration changed to meet the new technologies?

My traditional drawing has taken a dive in only one way: I now possess less artwork as whole pieces. Due to the compositional skills and speed of Photoshop, most of my print work is done in chunks, scanned, and composed onscreen. Over time, if I don't keep my eye on the ball, this process could erode my skill [of] compos[ing] as I draw.

Steffen Sauerteig, Svend Smital, and Kai Vermehr: a.k.a. eBoy

What are the three most recent jobs you've done?

We worked on a TV spot for a UK-based charity organization, finished a new 'Buildings' poster for our online shop, and created the poster for the launch of Adobe Air.

Which of these jobs were done for a venue or medium that was untraditional (not editorial)?

None of these jobs were editorial, but we usually work a lot for magazines.

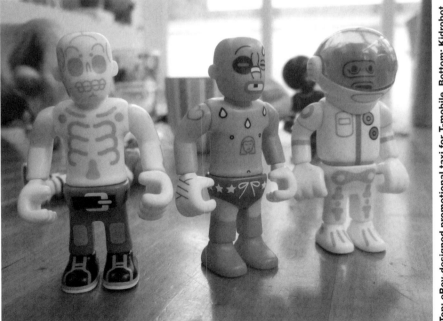

Top: eBoy-designed promotional taxi for T-mobile. Bottom: Kidrobot toys created by eBoy.

How much of your work is done for traditional (i.e., print) and untraditional (i.e., digital, toys, textiles, murals) media?

That's hard to tell; maybe 50/50?

What is the most challenging untraditional medium you've worked in?

Definitely the Peecol toy, as we had to re-learn Adobe Illustrator and delve into Modo, a 3-D application.

Who are your primary clients?

Magazines and advertising companies.

What new technologies have you had to master?

Our main tool has been and still is Photoshop, but for doing toys we [have] used Illustrator and toyed around with 3-D programs. Our hottest addition is 3-D software SketchUp from Google, [and] our latest one is Web-based group chat Campfire by 37signals. Oh, and Leap, an OS-X file browser, is our new archive browsing tool. I could also mention FFFFound, which is cool for recording your online image discoveries.

How has your illustration changed to meet the new technologies?

New communication tools help us to be faster—and optimizing our archive has been an ongoing struggle.

Susan Burghart: Primarily Digital

What are the three most recent jobs you've done?

I've recently done artwork for AT&T, McDonald's, and MasterCard.

Which of these jobs were done for a venue or medium that was untraditional (not editorial)?

AT&T's commission was for a primarily digital medium: to be used as cell phone wallpaper for AT&T phones.

How much of your work is done for traditional (i.e., print) and untraditional (i.e., digital, toys, textiles, murals) media?

Most of my work falls in the traditional realm; however, some of the visuals from the traditional print campaigns are carried over to the Web.

What is the most challenging untraditional medium you've worked in?

I find that whether or not the intended medium is traditional doesn't factor too much into how challenging a piece is for me as much as the complexity and concept do. I would have to say my most challenging piece was my artwork for MasterCard. This illustration was applied to print, but also used in a less traditional way: animated in Flash for the client's Web promotion. It was a very complex piece to illustrate, and given that it would be for a large audience, it was important that it be a carefully crafted piece.

Who are your primary clients?

[My] client list includes RED/Burton Snowboards, WGSN, Spunky Clothing UK, Womens Golf, Marie Claire (UK), Women's Weekly, British American Tobacco, Camel, Delta Airlines, AT&T, McDonald's, and MasterCard.

What new technologies have you had to master?

My illustration has always been primarily [in the] digital medium, so my goal is to stay knowledgeable about the latest versions of digital illustration software. I work primarily in Adobe Illustrator and Photoshop. I also like to dabble with Flash.

Susan Burghart illustration.

How has your illustration changed to meet the new technologies?

My work has actually shifted in recent years from purely digital vector work to adding in non-digital elements in a collage fashion to enhance my work and give it a more timeless feel. However, I find that I am still working in pure vector illustration more than I expected, as that generally is a smaller file size to transfer electronically, and is versatile in its application with both print and digital media.

Susie Jin: 100 Percent Printed

What are the three most recent jobs you've done?

1. *Color illustrations for a leveled reader,* The Smelly Sweatshirt, *written by Myka-Lynne Sokoloff (to be published by Pearson in 2010)*
2. *Illustration/design for Honeybear, a collection of twelve all-occasion pop-up cards, manufactured by Legacy Greeting Cards for release in January 2009*
3. *Writing/art for a children's gift board book titled* Good Table Manners for Little Monkeys

How much of your work is done for traditional (i.e., print) and untraditional (i.e., digital, toys, textiles, murals) media?

100 percent of my work is for printed products, mostly kids' books and licensed art projects in social expression/gift markets.

What is the most challenging untraditional medium you've worked in?

The Honeybear pop-up card collection was a challenge because I was responsible for all aspects of the project, from preliminary art sketches to final production files. While my art was traditional, made with gouache on paper, the 3-D format of the product was not. Pop-ups were new to me as well as to my manufacturer. By the time I had finished setting up the cards' production files and assembly instructions, I had grasped much of the fundamentals of paper engineering via a rocky, learn-as-you-go process. Creating the line from A to Z was quite an education.

Who are your primary clients?

Publishers and manufacturers that license my art [for use] on family-friendly products. I also freelance as a graphic designer.

What new technologies have you had to master?

Everything! Delivering artwork now spans the gamut, from preparing original art to be FedExed, to uploading to FTP sites and mailing CDs/DVDs. To be competitive in the art business, I market myself as a one-stop shop for ideas, art, and design. This requires proficiency on both Mac and IBM platforms, for programs such as Dreamweaver, Quark, Adobe Photoshop/Illustrator, Flash, a firm understanding of four-color process, etc., and I'm still learning!

How has your illustration changed to meet the new technologies?

Technology seems to speed up everyone's timetables, manufacturing rates and capabilities, and delivery schedules. I see new, innovative, illustrated products constantly turning over and fighting for shelf space. I strive to keep up with this pace to stay competitive and relevant in the market. This doesn't mean my illustration has necessarily changed, but my tools definitely have.

Whether I'm creating traditionally or digitally, I never want to [stop] retaining the hand-drawn soul of my images, so any project of mine always begins with a pencil sketch. For digital illustration work, I've outfitted my office

© Susie Lee Jin

Illustration by Susie Jin from *Good Table Manners for Little Monkeys.*

to keep me up-to-date, efficient, and prepared to address my clients' needs. I rely on my trusty scanner, fast Internet, inkjet/laser printers, Pantone color books, a huge Wacom screen with pen tool, multiple back-up drives and burners, art filing systems, several graphic programs, good lighting, and a very comfy office chair to get me through the day. This environment enables me to forget about any technological concerns and just focus on creating.

If I'm working traditionally, especially for commercial endeavors, I keep in mind to make the artwork so that that it can be cropped/applied on a range of printed products; after that, technology is the furthest from my mind. I create purely for the personal joy of making. In the end, I hope people emotionally connect to my images, rather than [to] any technology used to create or produce [them] as printed products.

Vince Kirsch: Same Old-Fashioned Materials

What are the three most recent jobs you've done?

A logo illustration for a copywriter to be used on Web site and collateral material, a black-and-white illustration to be used on Gourmet Garage tortilla chip packaging, and a color wall-covering design for Hospitality Wall-Covering company.

Which of these jobs were done for a venue or medium that was untraditional (not editorial)?

All three were not editorial.

How much of your work is done for traditional (i.e., print) and untraditional (i.e., digital, toys, textiles, murals) media?

I spend most of my time working on illustrations to appear in print, specifically children's books and newspapers.

What is the most challenging untraditional medium you've worked in?

Product packaging, because there are so many other elements to consider, such as typography, closure, bar codes, nutritional panels, and product display.

Who are your primary clients?

Publishers, newspapers, graphic designers, and Web site designers.

176

Illustration by Vince Kirsch.

What new technologies have you had to master?

Photoshop, and now [I] must tackle Illustrator.

How has your illustration changed to meet the new technologies?

It actually has not changed much at all, since I still do the actual artwork with [the] same old-fashioned materials that I always have.

Wes Bedrosian: 3-D Experiments

What are the three most recent jobs you've done?

Editorial pieces for Atlanta *magazine and the* Washington Post, *and several spots for the* Boston Globe.

177

Illustration by Wes Bedrosian.

How much of your work is done for traditional (i.e., print) and untraditional (i.e., digital, toys, textiles, murals) media?

All of my commissioned work is for editorial.

What is the most challenging untraditional medium you've worked in?

For my personal work, I am learning to make portraits with a 3-D sculpture program.

Who are your primary clients?

The Wall Street Journal, BusinessWeek, *the* New York Times, *the* Washington Post, Strategic Finance *magazine, and* Atlanta *magazine.*

What new technologies have you had to master?

Well, computer software (which includes Adobe Photoshop, SketchUp, Zbrush; e-mail, and e-mailing attachments), creating my own Web site, [and] managing my invoices with a database program. I also learned to draw on a Wacom screen. This has saved me a tremendous amount of time.

How has your illustration changed to meet the new technologies?

I use new technology primarily to meet faster deadlines. Both no and yes:

No: My traditional cross-hatch drawings with colored washes, which are now done entirely on the computer, are virtually identical to my traditional pen-and-ink wash drawings. I'm able to make them more elaborate in less time using new technology.

Yes: My new 3-D sculptures are a replacement [of] my acrylic-painted sculptures.

Yuko Shimizu: Billboards and Murals

What are the three most recent jobs you've done?

I have just finished working on three billboards for a beer advertisement in the UK, as well as five personal series illustrations for Microsoft's new Web site. I am working on a pro bono poster job in France for AIDS education for teenagers, along with regular editorial jobs I do monthly.

Which of these jobs were done for a venue or medium that was untraditional (not editorial)?

All of them are advertising in different media, so I would say they are untraditional.

How much of your work is done for traditional (i.e., print) and untraditional (i.e., digital, toys, textiles, murals) media?

Non-editorial jobs seem to be [increasing]. (In terms of whether my work is done traditionally or not, the answer is exactly half and half. Every job is half done by hand and half on the computer.) To be honest, at this point, a lot of untraditional jobs (other than advertising-related [ones] for larger corporations) are volunteer-based or for almost no pay. For me, most non-ad untraditional jobs are special projects to contribute to good causes. I try to balance ad work and editorial jobs, so I can take these jobs to give back. (For example, a mural project [I did] with Stefan Sagmeister and Robin Hood Foundation to help a school in a bad area of New York, and a toy design for Kidrobot to raise funds for the Save The Children Foundation. Both of them were either for no pay or a minimum payment.)

What is the most challenging untraditional medium you've worked in?

I have to say all the untraditional media are quite challenging. In editorial, I know pretty much how much time I need to finish what. It is very easy to predict. On the other hand, for untraditional jobs, every job needs a lot of research and planning because each one is so different.

For example, [the] mural I mentioned above was in such large-scale digital files, and figuring out how big to draw and how large to scan in and work on was a huge issue. At the end, I had to go into a client's office to use their machine that had a larger memory than my computer. Also, for the hand-painted Kidrobot toy, I needed to hire an assistant who knew a lot about the surface to work on sealing and priming the toy with special materials before I was even able to start. For the Microsoft Web site job, I had to use a PC, which I am not used to using, so learning all the functions, keys, and features took a while to get used to.

However, overall, it is a good balance between traditional (what I am used to) and untraditional (what I am not used to = challenge = stimulation, etc.).

Who are your primary clients?

[My clientele] is very diverse and hard to write out in short sentences. I would say some of my primary clients are editorial-based, such as Condé Nast, Rodale, Playboy, Outside, and others.

What new technologies have you had to master?

I keep track of all the new Adobe software (not necessarily to master them all, but at least [to] have them ready to open any files my clients would send me). My computer has to always be in the maximum RAM/memory to handle [the] ever-growing size of my digital illustration files, which is an average of about one or two GB per illustration now.

How has your illustration changed to meet the new technologies?

I started illustrating when the new computer technologies were already popular in the industry. I was lucky that it was not a huge adjustment using [the] computer. I am just getting more and more tech-y as years go by. [I] spend more and more money on computer hardware and software.

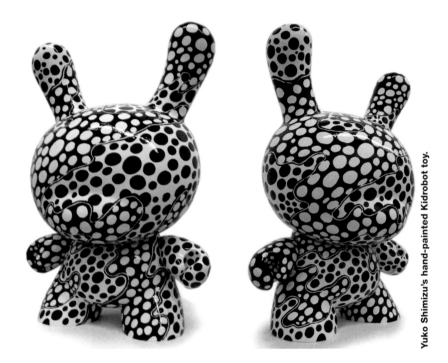

Yuko Shimizu's hand-painted Kidrobot toy.

Chapter Eight

The Perfect Portfolio

The Illustrator's Perspective

The definition of an illustration portfolio shifts as we explore the various facets of theory and practice, but that is not to say that there are no common denominators that apply generally.

Illustration is a figurative, not abstract, art form. Illustration does not encompass installation art or art that is not based in representation. The desire to create likeness goes back over 40,000 years ago when Shamans drew on cave walls. The drawings were illustrations, although we still know little more about their meaning since their discovery. It is, however, fair to say that these drawings of animals (principally horses, bison, mammoths, reindeer, and other large herbivores, but also some carnivores, such as bears and lions) are deeply rooted in magical or mythological beliefs that defy our comprehension. These illustrations were not mere decorations. They continue to express to us something real existing in ourselves, as they must have for those who created them thousands of years ago. They are visual aids much the same as the stained glass, frescos, mosaics, portraits, and sculptures of the great artists of the Middle Ages and the Renaissance, who were largely preoccupied with teaching the lessons of the Bible to the illiterate through their art. The intent of these artists was illustration's highest goal—to illuminate or make clear.

In the editorial market, freelance illustrators are hired to provide visual aids to sell magazines and accompany the text. Some illustrators are hired because they decorate pages, some illustrators are hired because they work hard at conceptually creating images that clarify the text, some illustrators are hired because they bring graphic commentary to the visual, and some illustrators are hired simply for style.

There is no single way to create the perfect portfolio. We would, however, suggest that the intent of the illustrator is the driving mechanism. From an illustrator's point of view, if your portfolio doesn't change as you change as an artist, then something is seriously wrong. Value judgments aside, here are some questions that might help you bring your portfolio into focus.

1. Do you seriously want to communicate something to other people?
2. Is your art an adventure into your own imagination and you don't care if other people understand it?
3. Is it your function as an artist to make the viewer see the world in your own way—not his way?
4. Do you like solving problems that are not your own?
5. Are you open to suggestions and willing to redo a piece to make the message clear?
6. Do you feel that your subject matter can be used with outside text?
7. Do you feel that what you have to say has significance?
8. Do you love the art-making process?
9. Do you want to be rich and famous?
10. Do you want to make magic?

Your portfolio is a portrait of who you are. You are not all things to all people; you have limitations. Picasso said, "Style is the by-product of our deficiencies."

We need to maintain a mobility of attitude, and a good sense of humor about ourselves will help us actually enjoy our creative journey and traveling time. I find I am more comfortable listening to my intuition than to theoretical debate. You already know the answers regarding your portfolio. You know where the drawing, painting, composition, and thinking are weak.

The Art Director's Perspective

Don't let anyone tell you there is no art in preparing a portfolio for an art director's perusal. As we've stated time and again throughout this book, the portfolio is your calling card; it must reflect precisely who you are, what you can do, and what you want to accomplish. Of course, this is an awful lot to ask of ten to fifteen images, but it is done all the time, and the sooner you develop a winning portfolio, the better your chances of success will be.

In that spirit, I will now describe the perfect portfolio I am waiting to see. The simple black case houses ten to fifteen pictures of original art, mounted or matted, of approximately the same size. When I open the portfolio, no pencils, paints, or egg-salad sandwiches fall out. The artist, male or female, is silent and lets the work do all the talking. Going through the work, I am filled with excitement, knowing that all of figurative art history has been absorbed and reformed to fit the person. The multiple stories I am being told are personal but familiar. Each portfolio piece builds upon and adds to the piece before it. There are single figures, people in groups, people inside, outside, and flying. As an observer I am looking up, looking down, moving in, and moving out.

The artist, a combination of DaVinici, Frida Kahlo, Josef Beuys, and numerous others, is fearless, taking on conceptual and pictorial problems for the sheer pleasure of combat. The drawing, painting, and thinking remain consistent throughout. There are line drawings and paintings that encompass a single message: Try me, I can do anything.

Art directors graze on portfolios., While some may show signs that viewing them is a burden, the fact is that without portfolios, art directors cannot function in one of their primary roles: making the best image. Here are some pointers for producing a striking portfolio.

What an art director wants to see in a portfolio starts with the word "professional." Whether you are presenting a digital or traditional (i.e., a book or case) portfolio, yours should look as though considerable forethought was put into the end product. This means the following:

1. Don't throw in work without forethought.
2. Don't provide more than fifteen images (or series of images).
3. Don't assume that anything will grab an art director's eye in a positive way simply because it's been published.

Here's the biggest "Don't": Don't think that because you make images, your talent is obvious to an art director. Even the most astute art directors need some help when it comes to looking at work. You can be a visual genius, but if your work is not presented well, it will be lost on all but the most scrupulous viewer. And since looking at a portfolio can be a very quick affair (usually measured in minutes), you must help the art director by editing your portfolio so that it tells a story—your story.

Here's what art directors want to see in a portfolio:

- Respect for one's own art (this means making a frame for your work that does not overpower it)
- A thematic or narrative thread (this does not necessitate having words throughout, but visually pairing or sequencing illustrations so the art director understands your point of view)
- The best work you've done (this may sound obvious, but is not always the case)
- Work that represents the work you want to get (this means if you are looking for editorial work, show a majority of that genre)
- Excellent reproductions (it is not necessary to show originals; in fact, in the digital age the definition of *original* has changed)
- A manageable presentation (a book should not be larger than 9×12 inches; a digital file should not be marred by glitches).
- Well-paced pages (art directors want to look forward to turning the pages).
- Confidence (the sum total of all these points should be an expression of confidence in your own work, and also in how you can execute your work in a professional context)

That said, don't allow these eight tenets to stifle your originality. Although a straightforward, unencumbered portfolio is a virtue, many memorable portfolios are smartly (and wittily) customized to exude personality. As long as the work is easy to see, the container in which it comes can be virtually anything, from elaborate wooden boxes to ornamented leather or metallic cases.

The media in which the work is showcased can also vary. Transparencies that are 4×5 or $2\frac{1}{4} \times 2\frac{1}{4}$ are always useful. Some illustration come equipped with a small light box for easy viewing. Color laser prints are the best bet (as long as the quality is good—when it's reproduced from a transparency, quality can be inferior). Originals are not always best to show (particularly if you want to use more than one portfolio), so good reproductions are a safe bet. Regardless of how it is displayed, the work must be clear and large enough to impress the viewer.

Then, of course, most of you will need a digital portfolio (addressed elsewhere in this chapter). Although most illustrators prefer to show traditional portfolios, many do show work on their laptops. This method is obviously great for those who do animation, but still imagery also looks great onscreen—sometimes better than in print.

The important thing to be aware of if you choose the digital format is that there are no glitches. Pre-launch your files right before your portfolio interview, or if you are sending a CD or DVD, make certain it plays on all computers. Similarly, if you are using a Web-based portfolio, make sure it launches without problems. Art directors are in impatient lot, and they do not have tolerance for things going wrong.

Finally, some will get personal appointments with art directors, while others will leave their portfolios for "drop-off." Still others will simply be asked to send a disc, or much more frequently, to provide a URL. If you get an appointment, here's what is expected of you:

1. Don't be in-your-face (be respectful of the art director's time and let the work do the talking).
2. Explain the work only if asked to do so (don't offer long narratives for everything you've done).
3. Don't bring drinks, food, or small animals into the interview (the last thing an art director wants is for you to slurp your iced coffee in her presence).
4. Don't pressure the art director for work; if an art director likes your work, you'll know it. If there is a chance that you will be commissioned, the art director will make that clear as well).
5. After the interview is completed, send a follow-up e-mail thanking the art director for his or her time.

Following these suggestions will not insure that you get work—the right time, the right place, etc., are still factors—but it will improve your professional standard.

Illustration With and Without a Computer

It is no longer possible to function as an illustrator without computer skills, even though illustrations are, in many instances, done by hand. Without knowledge of the computer (and all that it entails, including software, Web sites, and e-mail), you'll be stuck in the twentieth century. Nonetheless, without the hand skills of drawing and painting, the computer remains a tool incapable of telling a story or expressing an emotion. In making and marketing illustration, it is necessary to be both hand-savvy and computer-fluent.

To this end, in the MFA Illustration as Visual Essay department at the School of Visual Arts, we encourage students to maintain a balance. The following is an outline for the required computer portfolio class taught by Matthew Richmond that we hope will put this in perspective.

Computer Illustration Portfolio

As digital illustration processes proliferate, and the Internet as a tool continues to saturate not only the visual art world but also the entire world, an artist's education must include a firm foundation of not only "newer" mediums and techniques but also the unparalleled artistic and professional benefits these tools make available. The purpose of the Computer Illustration Portfolio class is to inspire and challenge students to comprehend, debate, and utilize new tools that will aid them in the creation of new work and/or assist them in producing and distributing their projects and ideas.

The course provides an extremely solid foundation, covering the origins, basic history, and logic of:

1. The Internet: including the Web, e-mail (e-mail clients), the domain registration process, the current global name-server system, file transfer, and peer-to-peer networking tools.
2. Hardware and Software: covering computer systems and accessories (scanners, drawing tablets, cameras, hard drives, portable music players, and media) as well as commercial and open-source applications and software packages.

Students receive advanced knowledge and hands-on training in:

1. Digital design and illustration tools and processes: including Adobe Photoshop, Adobe Illustrator, Macromedia Flash, type tools, and supporting utilities. All lectures, projects, and assignments are aimed at the needs of illustrators, and designers interested and involved with storytelling.
2. Self-promotion systems: discussions and projects will cover Web sites, online and offline mailing lists, postcards, business cards, promotional items, and all

corresponding workflows, including online file compression and processing as well as offset printing practices and tips.

3. Competent design: as the sole proprietor of his or her own individual online and offline visual identities, an illustrator needs to be somewhat of a jack-of-all-trades. Students will be educated in competent typeface selection and time-tested, grid-based layout and print designs.

The goal of the Computer Illustration Portfolio class is to alleviate the fear and frustration often associated with the complexity of computers by removing the computer from the beginning of creation process until such time that, together as a group, we learn how and why each individual student might utilize these newer mediums and techniques.

Chapter Nine

Teaching Illustration Today: The Nexus of Commerce and Education

Can the art of illustration be taught? Can the art of *marketing* illustration be taught? These are important concerns that go hand-in-glove. First, the field must be made crystal-clear to students. What it takes to pursue a career in the field must be equally understandable.

To learn more about how illustration is currently being taught, we interviewed four chairpersons of undergraduate illustration departments at Art Center, Maryland Institute College of Art (MICA), Parsons School of Design, and the School of Visual Arts (SVA), as well as the founder of the Center for Cartoon Studies. We asked them to weigh in on the state of the field from their perspectives and the role of the educator in its further growth and development.

During this period of change, the big question is, What should illustration students learn and what do they need to be artistically and business savvy in today's market? While these experts cover various approaches, all agree that illustration education is at a crossroads.

Steven Guarnaccia, Chair of BFA Illustration at Parsons School of Design

You are in the process of developing an undergraduate illustration program at Parsons School of Design. What is the biggest change you've experienced in illustration that impacts your curriculum?

The biggest change is the downturn in commissioned illustration work. Less work for illustrators in the field means fewer candidates entering the illustration program. As the field was seen to be less viable, interest in studying illustration, logically, fell off as well. The illustration department at Parsons went from being one of the biggest at the school to one of the smallest. And the students who did opt into the program were not always sure why they were there. They knew they wanted to draw and paint, and, besides the fine arts department, we were the only department that put an emphasis on those skills.

When we lecture to your illustration students, we routinely ask how many of them intend to enter the illustration field. Surprisingly, few raise their hands until we begin to specify among the different genres. What areas do your students most want to engage in after graduation?

I think one of the reasons for the response you describe is that, particularly when you and Marshall visited, the students were still part of the group that knew they wanted to study drawing and painting, but were either not aware of the range of illustration options open to them when they got out, or not necessarily interested in entering the field of illustration as it had become. Many students at that time wanted to become painters, or wanted to work as storyboard artists, or simply wanted an art school experience, but were planning to go on to do something entirely different when they got out of school. A few knew that there was interesting work out there for illustrators in Web design, animation, game design, illustration in the environment, and surface design. Now we're finding more and more students who are choosing to study illustration because they want to illustrate, and who are excited by the range of possibilities out there. These days, our students want to design commercial objects (I hesitate to say toys, because I think the toy market is, by its nature, a narrow and limited one, but certainly, that's currently the most attractive and visible area of illustrative objects), they want to publish their own books, [and] they want to make their images move.

192

Would you agree that editorial illustration is no longer the viable field it once was?

Editorial illustration is no longer the dominant area of activity for an illustrator as it once was. When I taught illustration at Parsons from 1981– 1991, if you said the word 'illustrator,' you meant editorial illustrator. Editorial illustration was the most personal and prestigious area of illustration, and it was also lucrative. It never could match advertising or corporate work for budgets, but the top editorial illustrators were doing very well indeed. I could confidently tell my students that there was enough work out there for each of them to expect a healthy career in editorial illustration. Of course, that took into account talent and desire. Even then, not everyone who came into the department had the will or desire to make it in the field. It was a predominantly freelance activity.

Now editorial illustration is only one of the many areas of activity available to an illustrator, and not always the most glamorous, challenging, or well-paying. Prices have stagnated, illustrators' creative autonomy has been tremendously curtailed, and the most exciting work out there is not necessarily being done for newspapers and magazines. So editorial is not producing the rock stars and role models for young illustrators that it once did.

How would you profile your current students? Why do they major in illustration and not design or other visual media?

First and foremost, our students express themselves most naturally through drawing and painting, whether using traditional or digital media. And they are interested in expressing something personal and unique to themselves. But we're training them to be visual communicators, and they are most interested in working in mass cultural media, whether on screens, walls, pages, or skateboards. They are not primarily thinking about gallery walls, though that's certainly what some of them aspire to, and it is within the range of creative options they're exposed to at Parsons. They tend to be self-motivated. I think to some degree, illustration students self-select. They—and this is a gross over-generalization—are often creative loners, following their own paths and working out solutions to creative problems individually rather than in teams. That said, our students go on to work for design and animation studios, as well as working freelance.

You are a veteran illustrator who has crossed platforms and media in many ways—from animation to editorial, from children's books to textiles. Do you inject this multi-disciplinary sensibility into your program? Do you encourage your students to move beyond illustration per se?

It's interesting—when I began designing rugs and hand-painting wooden toys, it was a fringe activity, an indulgence peripheral to my main activity as a print illustrator. Now the fringe has moved to center stage. Where in the '80s and '90s, a handful of illustrators also worked in these areas, now they are among the most vital and exciting areas of activity in the field. Our department is fundamentally based on the idea of [multi-disciplinary education]. It's what I felt was the essential direction of the field if it was to survive, and it's the basis for an education in any division or discipline at the New School. So we have students collaborating with jazz and animation students to create live images, music, and motion pieces; we have classes where writing students and comics students are working on visual narratives. Our toy class has collaborated with the design and technology department. We're currently restructuring the school so that disciplines will have even more opportunities to intersect and collaborate. It's how the world works, without lines drawn between kinds of experiences, and it's what the field of illustration looks like now.

Do you encourage your students to be "artists"?

I'm not sure I understand the question. We encourage the students to bring the highest level of visual thinking and technical skills to everything they do. I would say that all the arts require this of their practitioners. If you mean, Do we encourage students to be solely [inwardly] focused and unaware of the social or commercial implications of their work, we don't. Our students are most of all encouraged to be visual communicators.

What are the key illustration venues and markets, currently and over the next five years?

I think that motion is the new print. Narrative forms of all sorts have a tremendous ability to communicate. Animation, comics and graphic novels, visual journalism, performance, illustration, [and] children's books are all areas that I think will be viable culturally and economically into the future.

194

If you were making a pitch to prospective students of your program, what would it be?

We're living in a world immersed in visual media. Much of this visual culture is drawn, invented, and imagined. New forms are born with great frequency—our students are giving rise to many of them. What could be more exciting and more personally satisfying than to participate in our collective culture in such a direct and fundamental way?

Whitney Sherman, Chair of BFA Illustration at Maryland Institute College of Art (MICA)

How many of your students take illustration as a major?

My students are all illustration majors, but if the question is really meant to determine why students major in illustration, I think it is because they are eager to articulate the world, love to draw, and love stories of all kinds.

Has this changed over the past decade since the advent of digital art and design?

Digital art and design has changed the aesthetic (also affected by social and economic concerns) of work and made replicating traditional styled works easier to modify. The other changes are more rapid exchange of ideas and [distribution of] work, and more experimentation. They have more access to the public in ways that give feedback, community, and income.

What are the traditional courses you offer?

MICA Illustration offers 'Media Kitchen: Wet'; 'Media Kitchen: Dry'; 'Collage'; and a flexible course called, 'Studio Remix' where faculty are selected based on their materials use and methods. Students learn the materials skills through in-class workshops and learn how and why the faculty works in these materials, which are usually very different than what the students normally use. Recent remixes included working with wood on the story The Lion and the Mouse *with Philadelphia artist Shelley Spector, working collaboratively with a combination of digital and traditional printmaking with Nick Karvonis and New York guest artist John Rappelye, and working with found objects with French artist Alain Corbel.*

The college also offers traditional courses in printmaking, ceramics, painting, drawing, and fibers, which students frequently access.

What are the untraditional courses?

If untraditional classes are digital or digital/traditional combinations, MICA Illustration offers the following: a freshman elective called 'Digital as Illustration,' which introduces students to the language of illustration using only digital tools and applications; 'Digital Illustration,' which is a primer on basic digital applications like Photoshop, Illustrator, and Painter; 'Advanced Photoshop Techniques,' which digs deeply into Photoshop skills to have students emerge being able to use this application in very sophisticated ways, either as direct drawing ([with] Cintiq/Wacom tablets) or in coloring of hand-drawn imagery.

We also consider the 'Studio Remix' class as a place for non-traditional media use. Since the faculty and the media used change, this course gives a lot of flexibility to shape what materials students work in, to open their eyes to alternatives.

In the school at large, the course 'High Touch Meets High Tech' was developed by an illustration faculty member for the general fine art department to help break the phobias of digital media, but the course has endured as a model for transitioning between digital manipulation and traditional mark-making.

With the demise of editorial illustration, what is your primary focus?

We are not limiting our focus to specific markets; rather, MICA Illustration focuses on developing students who have multiple skill sets to remain fluid and adaptable in an ever-changing marketplace and who creatively solve problems.

Fundamental skills like drawing and narrative/storytelling (such as in picture books); understanding literary metaphors, perspectives, and pacing; and conceptual/problem-solving skills (as in sequential art, theater sets, and concept art for film) keep students relevant and able to transpose their best skills to any number of positions.

We tell them we can't predict the future markets in illustration, so they have to be ready to be artists, thinkers, and writers.

Do you find that students are anxious about the future?

Yes, they are. I sometimes think this is because they (or their parents) have spent so much money in four years. The debt burden is high. Other times I think it is their global awareness or fear of the complexities of the world—changes [with] the economic landscape, the amount of information they need to absorb to be 'informed,' and so on.

In terms of art making, they don't seem to have anxiety at all; they have the same intense interest in making illustration and finding ways to get them out in public. I don't think they can imagine illustration not existing. Even if it is called something else, the urge is still the same.

What are your students' primary concerns?

Their concerns are with access to resources (they want to play and work, and they get frustrated when they can't try things out or have limited access to interesting tools) and restrictions on their work or on their lifestyle (copyright, limited former markets, and the ability to support themselves soon after school).

Who do your students look towards as models of practice for the future?

They see collectives, either virtual or actual, as really viable means to their futures. Commerce and social sites both give them the range and flexibility to accomplish this. Collectives also give them the freedom to form artistic and commercial alliances to respond to bigger projects or projects that exceed their skill sets.

The DIY movement provided an interest in limited-edition artists' works. Even though the consumer was not really, 'doing it themselves,' they were made more appreciative of the hand-crafted object.

Do you find that students are studying design, typography, motion, etc., as adjuncts to their illustration coursework?

Some are and some aren't. [Having been] a designer for many years, having faculty trained in photography does bring a different perspective to our students' experience. We also have found a heightened interest in letterforms with the 'Hand Letters' class—less formal study and [more] practice with letters.

We do also have a lot of 'slash' students who have an interest in two or more areas of study. Many are interested in both illustration and design or illustration and animation. MICA has programs of declared concentrations in Book Arts, Graphic Design, Animation, Video, Painting, and Printmaking. These concentrations allow us to extend the ability to feed the students' academic desires and to build on IL programming.

Would you agree there is something called "The New Illustration"?

Yes, I think illustration has gone wild, which has had an influence on what is expected from illustrators by art directors, designers, and the public. We are seeing work that might have been considered too experimental years ago—a little more personal than universal.

What would you say it is?

The new illustration is about personal voice. It has become desirable from both the practitioner's and the client's perspectives. It is also emerging out of personal works in sketchbooks, exhibitions, and self-published works; perhaps out of frustration of shrinking or non-existent markets, or from new technology's low distribution costs.

How do you prepare your students for the demands of the new illustration market?

Strong fundamental skills, a culture that supports variety in voice/expression, awareness of today, learning opportunities, and lots of professional development.

Along these lines, have there been any attempts to merge other courses (design, motion, advertising, etc.)?

Not merge so much as collaborate . . . and find outside opportunities to connect with, find opportunities within the college to connect ideas and making.

What do you currently look for in an incoming student?

Students who are smart, who read and draw, can be taught to be highly skilled illustrators; but without drive and passion, students can't live on reading and drawing alone. We look for students who are verbal. Not everyone embodies all these things, but the students know we value these attributes. More and more, their networking skills are also becoming important. The lone illustrator model is becoming extinct.

What do the incoming students look for in your program?

Resources, access to faculty and faculty's professional contacts, and community. They come to MICA because of the close learning and professional relationships they can form with faculty.

Ann Field, Chair of Illustration at Art Center in Pasedena, California

How many of your students take illustration as a major?

Illustration is the largest department at Art Center: five hundred-plus students in a school of thirteen hundred.

198

Has this changed over the past decade since the advent of digital art and design?

Illustrators need to have more adaptable skills to survive.

What are the traditional courses you offer?

Head painting, figure painting, comp and painting, perspective, and anatomy.

What are the untraditional courses?

'Mixed Up (mixing digital with hand)', 'Supersized' (three-dimensional solutions to illustrated ideas), portfolio design lab (high-grade art-directed portfolio production), and 'Storyboarding for Motion.'

With the demise of editorial illustration, what is your primary focus?

Entertainment work for feature animation and a hybrid 'illustration/design' of illustration skills and design practices.

Do you find that students are anxious about the future?

Not really; they are excited about the opportunities. They have no recollection of a traditional past.

What are your student's primary concerns?

Fees and keeping the flow of work going.

Who do your students look toward as models of practice for the future?

National Forest, a young illustration team that works collaboratively and does a lot of advertising work (alums), and superstars like Yuko Shimizu; also, Pixar animators like alum Thea Kratter.

Do you find that students are studying design, typography, motion, etc., as adjuncts to their illustration coursework?

Yes; they want to, and in fact, are creating hybrid majors. Illustration classes are 50 percent and motion or design classes make up the remaining 50 percent.

How do they fulfill this? Are type and motion classes offered?

Graphic design classes and motion classes are available to illustrators at Art Center, and they have to take them in sequence with all the prerequisites as designers do.

Do you see students using their illustration skills as a basis for other disciplinary work?

The crossover between illustration and gallery is prevalent on the West Coast. The biggest correlation between disciplines is where illustration and motion collide—where there is a huge need for illustrative imagery.

Would you agree there is something called "The New Illustration"?

Yes, my program is titled just that: 'New Illustration.'

What would you say it is?

A sense of being able to identify where your work is going and the possibilities inherent in it: Is it for publishing work? Could it go to motion? Can you design a toy? Are you able to publish a' zine?

How do you prepare your students for the demands of the "new illustration" market?

'Business 101,' a full-term intensive class and portfolio design lab with regular guest speakers. [The students] learn about the vicissitudes of the market—what segment demands what kind of special attention—and how to network with art directors and art buyers.

What do you currently look for in an incoming student?

Ideas and drawing skills: strong traditional skills are still paramount; life drawings and sound understanding of anatomy coupled with drawing from observation will serve any student at Art Center who enters the illustration department and then can opt for any area of focus.

Can you describe the ideal portfolio for an incoming student?

Fifteen to twenty life drawings, a good self-portrait from observation in color, a two-year sketchbook, and some conceptual color work.

What do the incoming students look for in your program?

Drawing skills taught to a high level of finish and the assurance of some kind of creative career.

And can you describe the ideal portfolio for a graduating student?

One that represents his or her creative voice and is definitive, executed to a high level of professional finish and presentation.

Thomas Woodruff, Chair of BFA Illustration at School of Visual Arts in New York

How many of your students take illustration as a major?

There are presently 436 students enrolled in the illustration/cartooning department. To characterize all their motives would be foolhardy. The constants appear to be that they are looking for picture-making skills, and to convey content and narrative with images. Other than that, each seems to have a different agenda, be it editorial, fantasy, gallery, production design, science fiction, children's books, tattooing . . . the list could go on and on.

Has this changed over the past decade since the advent of digital art and design?

The most common ground with the students in this department is that the advent of digital art and design is suspect. This is a generation that broke its eye teeth during the digital craze, and many of these students (although they know all the digital moves) are tired of the look, and wish to do something primarily by hand. The cool detachment inherent in digital art has few adherents with the new generation, and this has changed in the past several years. Many of my advanced electives employing digital methods fail to run due to poor enrollment.

What are the traditional courses you offer?

We offer the traditional courses involving drawing, painting, conceptual problem solving, etc., and advanced electives in children's books, caricature, science fiction and fantasy, fashion, humor—oh, the laundry list again!

What are the untraditional courses?

We do an unusual junior thesis project, theme-based (and the theme changes every year, e.g., 'Kings and Queens,' 'Location as Character,' 'Classical Myths Transformed,' 'Beautiful Losers'). This course also has a companion course in the humanities. The goal is to ask these young artists to find their inspiration in cultural sources outside of their own imagination and to learn how to develop a significant body of work, fueled by research. This project gives our students a leg up on their competition, for they learn how to become fluid in relation to the past history of imagery—a thing that is sorely lacking in our new generation—rather than to stress the new-fangled gizmos. It also asks them at an early age to work on an extended project, different from most illustration programs, which are a collection of varied assignments.

With the demise of editorial illustration, what is your primary focus?

To paraphrase Mark Twain, its death has been highly overrated! Illustration is alive and, if not totally well in relation to magazines, it is morphing and thriving in interesting ways. Problem-solving and picture-making will never have a 'demise.' To structure a college curriculum around a trend is a disastrous practice in my opinion. I do not mean this in a conservative way; rather, it seems radical to educate the innovators and not the imitators. The trend may be to say that editorial illustration is dead, but painting died in the seventies when I was in art school, and it seems rather robust! I remember in 1977 being corralled on benches in the back of the Museum of Holography in SoHo (now long gone). The director told us to drop our brushes and to take on the new mantle of the contemporary artist.

Do you find that students are anxious about the future?

All twenty-somethings are anxious. Are they optimistic? Yes. Do they have reason to be? If they are canny, hard-working, and reliable, in my opinion, yes, they do. The SVA team of working faculty trains the students in how to behave, stifle their privileged tendencies, and act like pros. If they can do this, normal anxiety about entering the work force is substantially minimized, as they will be wanted in the world.

What are your student's primary concerns?

They want to know how to maintain a sense of self in a corporate culture. They want to know how to create edgy works that may not bring financial gain. They want to know how to afford to live in a major city like New York after graduation without a trust fund. They wonder if they have the fortitude to really be artists. These concerns are not easily answered—I ask many of the same [questions] almost daily.

Who do your students look toward as models of practice for the future?

It changes by the month. Young artists are fickle and they fall in love easily. [Some look to the] fantasy folk feature Franzetta, some vibrate with James Jean, the entrepreneurial types think Shephard Fairey is the bee's knees, Peter de Seve is revered, Chris Ware rules... it seems to depend a lot on someone's last book or last exhibition. You want to hear something curious? Almost every student I have had in the past four years would put Jim Henson's and Brian Froud's Dark Crystal *on their top ten movie list. This film was made before most of them were born. Go figure!*

Do you find that students are studying design, typography, motion, etc., as adjuncts to their illustration coursework?

Of course, and there are also students who study portrait painting, sculpture, puppetry, printmaking, [and] stop-motion animation. We recently did independent study courses in shoe design and in high-fashion makeup with particular students. Look, I never took an illustration course in college. I took painting and video. Steve Brodner, an instructor here and perhaps the hardest-working illustrator in America, also never studied illustration specifically, but we both had educations that taught us how to solve visual problems. Out of school, I worked in avant-garde theatre and did storyboards. Steve did caricatures at parties. My predilection was literary, his political. We found our ways in the world by incorporating our interests. If a student is socially awkward, his or her chances of becoming a freelance artist are much [smaller] than it he or she is gregarious. It does not matter how many typography or motion graphics courses they take.

Would you agree there is something called "The New Illustration"?

No. I can divide most of the work in annuals like American Illustration *into three categories: the good-bad draftsman, the retro-collage, and the computer-colored ink drawing (a.k.a., the school of Istvan Banyai). These are stylistic trends, not a movement, and they already feel a bit dated to my students.*

What would you say it is?

Technology is determining the look du jour, and that is unfortunate. High-res files are cheap and efficient, and everyone is trying their best. Soon technology will advance so other, less flat styles come back into vogue. The big problem with illustration is the paycheck. Fees have remained stagnant for decades, so it tends to be appropriate for the younger artists, and the older ones need to find higher-paying work.

How do you prepare your students for the demands of the "new illustration" market?

As I said above, it will change before their skin totally clears up. They know what they need to know for what they want to do, or the world will present them with something new.

Along these lines, have there been any attempts to merge other courses (design, motion, advertising, etc.)?

These questions all seem to be leading in a screwy direction. Do I think every illustrator needs to study typography? No; only if they are inclined. Same goes for motion graphics, ICAD, and any other programs that will not save lives. When I took my position as chair, I spoke with Carol Devine Carson, the genius head of design at Knopf books, a woman whose exquisite eye is unmatched. She said [whom] she hired the most were hand-letterers. I feel we are too quick to buy into the next new technology when they are only programs. How many times have you seen a blockbuster with fabulous CGI and realized that the effects artists didn't know the rules of warm and cool light? I see it all the time. I would only hire a designer who loves type (and I have met many), not someone who studied it to get a low-paying job right out of college. We try constantly creating new courses to reflect market trends. Some pull students, some don't. The advanced students have few required courses and they can take classes in other departments. Most of our students know that they can 'draw' themselves into success.

What do you currently look for in an incoming student?

We look for the best and the brightest, obviously. We look for those who not only have a technical bent but also wish to become culturally sophisticated and contribute to our visual culture. As I stated before: innovators, not imitators.

What do the incoming students look for in your program?

They look for expansion and growth. Often these students have very limited experiences when it comes to the arts. Most of their image vocabularies come from TV and movies, and many have never been to a museum, let alone a concert hall. Being in New York is a serious leap into culture for most of these young artists. Our faculty are all successful professionals as [opposed to] most other colleges. Yes, the students want to know the tricks of the trade (as do all art majors and, in fact, all college students). But I feel SVA's incoming students are looking for something more…a way to enter into the cultural dialog, become players in the world we live in, and influence the way we see the world and the way the world looks.

James Sturm, Founder of the Center for Cartoon Studies

You are the first person to open a school exclusively for cartoon studies. This must mean you see a future in the field. What kind of future do you see?

Part of the motivation of starting the Center for Cartoon Studies was to create a program where cartooning was considered a legitimate artistic pursuit and was not so tightly tethered to commercial art. I thought it would be helpful for emerging cartoonists to have the same space at a pivotal point in their artistic journey that a poet or sculptor is afforded at an MFA program.

I think there is always a future for well-constructed stories. As forces in our culture aggressively bombard us with images, cartooning is a great way to shape meaning by arranging images to make sense of the world.

What do you require of an incoming student? What experience? What talent?

We require maturity. CCS is a tiny community in a small village. What many undergraduate colleges can tolerate in regards to typical freshman behavior, CCS can not. Most of our students are a bit older. The few students we have accepted right out high school are preternaturally mature. Now that CCS can offer an MFA, it helps attract more mature students.

As it enters its fourth year, CCS is requiring more of its incoming students, because it's getting more competitive to get in. This is the first year we have a waiting list. Students submit all the usual stuff—an essay, letters of recommendation, some portfolio samples—[plus] a 3–5 comic featuring themselves, a piece of fruit, a snowman, and a robot. This comic is the most telling aspect of their application. It showcases drawing, design, production, and writing skills. Comics have come in that were hastily copied or stunningly presented. Starting this year, with students we are unsure about, we ask them to resubmit their comic. This revision request provides an opportunity to see how open the applicant is to revision and feedback.

Cartooning is labor-intensive, so we will look for experiences that speak to the ability to follow through with a project. I also look for curiosity. It's great when students are interested in a lot of different stuff and not just comics.

Talent is a funny word. Lots of elements can make up for a lack of what is traditionally thought of as 'talent': doggedness, smarts, patience, etc.

What do you teach them once they are students?

CCS's curriculum focuses on process. There are so many stages of crafting a comic—from generating ideas to preparing files to send to a printer. CCS teaches it all. From the very first assignment, students have to make multiple copies so they understand that a finished project is the printed page. I am amazed by how many books, 'zines, and mini-comics the first three classes have generated. Nothing beats seeing your work in print, and CCS encourages a DIY mentality (and has a great production lab for student use).

Is the business of cartooning one of your curricula offerings?

Yes. The second year, there is a professional practices class. We cover contracts, creating letterhead/ID, invoicing, preparing book proposals, and applying for grants. We also bring in book agents and, every spring, have an editor's day where editors review student work. Last year's professional practices class saw CCS sponsor the New York Center for Independent Publishing (NYCIP) symposium. Students created a promotional brochure for every attendee (which included a lot of movers and shakers in the publishing world) and manned tables at the event.

How does a comic artist address business, and how do they market their wares?

Understanding business, at the very least, helps [artists] re-calibrate their expectations. As we both know, students don't always possess the most realistic expectations concerning the business end of things. Certainly the more you know, the less you can be taken advantage of. The 'Professional Practices' class is crucial to the curriculum but also one of the hardest to teach because you want to nurture the students and not be a 'dream killer.'

206

And speaking of business, do you believe there will be a point of saturation in this one?

Mediocrity and schlock has saturated every business! Graphic novels will continue to grow for a while still. [They are] part of of the publishing landscape of the 'big houses,' and there is no going back.

What do you recommend students do to insure their futures?

Love what you do or do something else.

Do all your students pursue comics and cartooning, or is this a "liberal arts" for visual art?

This is a great question. I do think of cartooning as the 'liberal arts' for visual art. All of our students consider themselves cartoonists, but the field overlaps so many others. A cartoonist could create children's books or have his or her work hang in art galleries. [Cartoonists] could do political cartooning for a newspaper, draw superheroes, or work in a more literary vein. My education as a cartoonist has honed skills that have allowed me to write for periodicals, develop television shows, and art direct a newspaper.

Afterword

Rumors of the Death of Illustration Have Been Greatly Exaggerated

Dire predictions of editorial illustration's death (some of them made by us) may be more delusion than reality. All you have to do is page through the current crop of American magazines to find new names attached to numerous conceptual images. Despite a dearth of the mammoth tableau—single- and double-page spreads and covers that were once the cornerstone of American illustration—by America's most illustrious illustrators, threats of demise have not diminished the sheer volume of young artists producing some of the most eclectic illustrations ever. The work may be physically smaller in overall reproduction size, but illustrators today are more prodigious than a decade ago.

Many of this number are finding alternative outlets for their work—toys, games, animation, even tableware—but given our survey of illustrators about traditional versus nontraditional, it is clear that editorial is still the favored genre. Despite the allure of motion, the expansiveness of graphic novels, and the joy of three-dimensional objects, the traditional, single-image editorial format continues to be the most effective means of reaching an audience. An editorial illustrator may not always be the muse-driven author of independent ideas, but the medium allows for individual personalities to emerge, for intelligence to shine, and even for innovation to peek through from time to time.

The new American illustrators are not wed to a national style as they were during the Rockwell '40s and '50s, but many share certain visual and conceptual similarities. Humor (often subtle, occasionally satiric) is a consistent feature, and probably one of the most difficult conceits to do well. Also, rather than exacting and detailed renderings, new drawing methods are loose and sketchy with an expressionist sensibility, or resolutely mechanical in an ironically faux-anonymous manner. Graphic and typographic design are also factors in some work. Perhaps a debt is owed to Barbara Kruger, Jenny Holzer, or Lawrence Weiner, or maybe the rationale for alternative methods is simply a quest for new ways to make illustration accessible to a broad public. These days, words—scrawled, scripted, and typeset—are prevalent.

The space allotted to illustration has shrunk in direct proportion to limited amounts of editorial space in most magazines and newspapers, owing, in large part, to steady decreases in advertisements and increases in printing and production costs. While this is not a positive portend, it is also nothing new. Illustration has long suffered the vicissitudes of the market and the ravages of the economy. What it means is that illustrators have adapted to survival in a Darwinian way. They have become more minimalist in form and content in order to communicate in smaller spaces, void of visual effluvia. Therefore, shorthand is required, with clarity and eloquence the goal.

Some old-school critics argue that these minimalist illustrators are "rough and raw" because they just don't know how to draw. That is a fallacy. The notion that traditional drawing skills have atrophied and are no longer valued by those who teach or purchase illustration couldn't be more ridiculous. Drawing will always be a virtue. However, classical rendering—realism and surrealism—is no longer the standard by which to judge art. And illustration, which sometimes serves as a marker of where art is headed, has simply adapted.

While some art directors prefer photography, there has been a recent surge in art directors who have keen illustration preferences and have opened the pages of venerable newspapers and magazines—including the *New Yorker*, the *New York Times*, and *Time*—to the new illustration. While some of the old guard is still very active, the twenty-somethings are contributing timely visual points of view. Each has a distinct method, but all are connected to the zeitgeist. And there's nothing better than that good old zeitgeist.

If this is a short chapter, dispelling the rumors of illustration's demise doesn't need much more attention.

Web Directory

Artists' Web Sites

Peruse these pages for inspiration on how to set up your online portfolio.

www.marshallarisman.com
This site showcases the artist's paintings and illustrations, with emphasis on the latter. Slide shows and Flash animations are used to optimum effect. However, this site does not offer current-events information, so it requires less attention than the next.

www.viktorkoen.com
As a resource for the art buyer, this site offers a variety of archival and current information, including notices of book signings and other promotional events. Just remember, when doing a site this layered, don't forget to continually update the "news."

www.mirkoilic.com/start.html
This site is designed to highlight illustration and design, as well as a smattering of interactive work. The disciplines are represented separately but equally. Each section requires clicking on various examples, which are not annotated, but the images speak for themselves. The access is fairly easy.

www.davidsandlin.com/index.html
This appropriately gaudy site is a billboard for the artist's various exhibitions. Its garish design is the perfect complement to Sandlin's raw style. While the main sell is his gallery work, for the art buyer there are also pages for current work, news, and biography.

http://maryjovath.com
This conservatively designed site provides the user with the basic information, an archive of visuals, and a bibliography. The transparency of the layout allows the work to take center stage.

www.gregoryacrane.com
This is a typical artist's site. The work takes center stage, and there are very few bells and whistles, but there are background hues that are not necessary. Be careful of how you frame your work.

www.garypanter.com/index.html
Few things are more fun than Gary Panter's work, and this site is a perfect evocation of his sensibility. The spinning Panter globe in the corner is just the right touch. No need for excess animation.

www.rabidrabbit.org
This site is for a collective of artists who contribute to the print 'zine *Rabid Rabbit*. The site is used to describe and sell the publication but also highlight the contributors. If you contribute to publications, make sure your own Web site is advertised, too.

www.laurenredniss.com
This elegantly designed site is used to sell Redniss' book and showcase her *New York Times* work. PDFs of reviews of her work, which are useful for prospective art buyers, are available on the site.

www.domandk.com
This joint portfolio site directs the user to individual portfolio pages. As long as the sites are distinct, sharing a URL can be beneficial.

www.yukoart.com
This side provides all the information a successful illustrator needs. The work is clearly visible and the news and press information is there for whoever needs to see it.

http://wendikoontz.com

This is one of the most joyous sites we've seen. Its fun design immediately suggests that the artist has a choice sense of humor. Making a site personal can be a virtue.

www.ayakakeda.com

A user can't help but want to enter this illustrator's site after seeing the witty, pop-up home page.

www.johnhendrix.com

In addition to a wonderfully appealing graphic presentation, this site contains a blog that is useful to friends, fans, and art buyers.

www.sampaints.com

This site is functional, but without the name of the artist prominently displayed, it is easy to be confused. The second page of the site, with examples shown, is much more efficiently designed.

Interviewee Web Sites

A limited selection of the personal Web sites of our interviewees, as well as sites on which their work appears. Check them out for some insight into their careers and creative lives.

Gary Baseman
www.garybaseman.com

Tim Biskup
www.timbiskup.com

Paul Budnitz
www.kidrobot.com

André Carrilho
www.videojackstudios.com

Byron Glaser and Sandra Higashi
www.zolo.com/fun.html

James Jean
www.prada.com

Geoff McFetridge
www.championdontstop.com

Wendy Plovmand
www.wallcollection.com

Toy Sites

Visit these sites for more information on designer toys:

VinylPulse.com
www.vinylpulse.com

MyPlasticHeart.com
www.myplasticheart.com

Artoyz.com
www.artoyz.com

The Toy Association of Southern California:
www.tasc-toys.com

Canadian Toy Association:
www.cdntoyassn.com

China Toy Association:
www.toy-cta.org

Sonos Product Development
www.sonosproductdevelopment.com

Annuals

Here is a list of the most popular annuals in the United States (others abound in Europe and Asia). Entry fees, deadlines, and other information are available on the publications' respective Web sites:

Society of Illustrators Annual
www.societyillustrators.org

American Illustration Annual
www.ai-ap.com

Communication Arts Annual
www.commarts.com

Print Magazine Annual
www.printmag.com

3×3 Magazine Annual
www.3x3mag.com

Society of Publication Designers Annual
www.spd.org

Art Directors Club (ADC) Annual
www.adcglobal.org

Alternative Web sites

The following are a few alternative Web sites, among many, that offer a variety of services.

The Alternative Pick

www.altpick.com

Altpick.com is an essential tool for the working artist. Artists of all types use Altpick. com as a place to show samples of their work and to reach viewers who can purchase their services. The site is built to allow each member direct, real-time access twenty-four hours a day, seven days a week. Members have the ability to make unlimited changes and updates to images and personal information. They can post images in JPEG and GIF formats, QuickTime and MPEG videos, animation, and Flash and Director files. Members who have their own Web sites will get a boost in traffic from their links at Altpick.com. Artists who don't have their own Web sites appreciate the ease and simplicity of the site. It is an affordable way to create a Web presence without having to build a site from scratch. Each member has his or her own unique Web address (*www. altpick.com/artistsname*).

Buyers use Altpick.com to discover new artists and see the latest work. They stay informed about industry events, shows, and happenings. They can keep their own favorites and notes using a feature called "my altpick." The site reflects the personality and approach of *The Alternative Pick* (the book) and yet is a unique entity all its own.

A page on *www.altpick.com* costs $299 per year, and allows you to:

- Display and change up to ten multimedia files at any time
- Add up to three links to any other sites
- Receive e-mail directly from the site
- Enter key words that will help the site's viewers find you using the search or advanced search functions
- List biographical information or thoughts about your work
- Inform users automatically when you have made changes to your page
- Post classified and job listings
- Have news items as well as calendar items about you listed on the site
- Promote yourself each time you update your work

The i-spot

www.theispot.com

In the twelve years since its inception, the goal of Theispot.com has been to build an online home for illustrators where they can not only market their work cost-effectively, but can also communicate with other artists worldwide. According to Theipsot.com, "We continually reshape the Web site to answer the changing needs of both our subscribing illustrators and the many art buyers that have made Theispot.com their primary illustration Web resource. Today Theispot.com showcases the work of artists from dozens of countries, serves buyers internationally, and is widely recognized as the world's premier illustration site."

Using the online upload tool, illustrators submit their eighteen images, contact information, and key words directly to the Theispot.com database for each assignment portfolio. Buyers can search the entire database using key words that reference style, subject, and medium, or they can select the portfolios of specific illustrators or representative groups. The buyer contacts the artist or rep directly via phone, fax, or e-mail, to discuss and assign the job.

Illustrators upload their work using an online tool, following the provided guide for key-wording, and specifying any previous usages or restrictions on their work. Theispot.com requires that the work be formatted in both high and low resolution, and displays the low-res image on the site and archives the high-res version. The key words for each image are entered into Theispot.com's database, and the artist then selects from ten price levels to price his work appropriately for certain simple licensing usages. Buyers can search for illustrations by key word or, if they prefer, they can view the entire stock collection of a specific artist.

Illoz

www.illoz.com

Illoz.com is a portfolio site for illustrators that doubles as a very useful workspace for art directors. The idea is to establish a new and better way for art directors to find and interact with illustrators. Illoz.com was created by two guys with an idea: the same two odd-balls who brought Drawger.com (a blog-hosting site for illustrators) to life. Illoz.com is a portfolio site for illustrators that is by invitation only, so not everyone who wants a portfolio site there will be able to get one. Numbers are limited to keep the quality high. The cost is $150 per year, but it's free to test-drive for sixty days. For art directors to get the very most out of Illoz.com, getting an account there is a must. Projects can be taken from start to finish, right there at the site, from viewing sketches online to downloading the final art.

Because art director accounts at Illoz.com provide access to a confidential area of the site that portfolio owners do not have access to, art directors have to either receive an invitation from an art director with an existing account or apply for an account.

Children's Illustrators

www.childrensillustrators.com

This is a resource and online community of over seven hundred illustrators, sixteen agents, and almost 20,000 illustrations. It is scanned daily by art buyers from international "publishing houses, advertising agencies, and design groups." There is a subject gallery, a style and medium gallery, an agent showcase, and a newsletter. The portfolio gallery allows a wide range of approaches and images to be seen, and a section on published books provides up-to-date information.

Index

Books from Allworth Press

Allworth Press is an imprint of Allworth Communications, Inc. Selected titles are listed below.

Starting Your Career as a Freelance Illustrator or Graphic Designer, Revised Edition
by Michael Fleishman (paperback, 6 × 9, 272 pages, $19.95)

Inside the Business of Illustration
by Steven Heller and Marshall Arisman (paperback, 6 × 9, 256 pages, $19.95)

Business and Legal Forms for Illustrators, Third Edition
by Tad Crawford (paperback, 8 ½ × 11, 160 pages, $29.95)

The Education of an Illustrator
edited by Steven Heller and Marshall Arisman (paperback, 6 ¾ × 9 ⅞, 288 pages, $19.95)

Teaching Illustration: Course Offerings and Class Projects from the Leading Undergraduate and Graduate Programs
edited by Steven Heller and Marshall Arisman (paperback, 6 × 9, 288 pages, $19.95)

Your Career in Animation: How to Survive and Thrive
by David B. Levy (paperback, 6 × 9, 256 pages, $19.95)

Animation: The Whole Story, Revised Edition
by Howard Beckerman (paperback, 6 ⅞ × 9 ¼. 336 pages, $24.95)

The Education of a Comics Artist
by Michael Dooley and Steven Heller (paperback, 6 × 9, 288 pages, $19.95)

The Business of Being an Artist, Third Edition
by Daniel Grant (paperback, 6 × 9, 352 pages, $19.95)

Legal Guide for the Visual Artist, Fourth Edition
by Tad Crawford (paperback, 8½ × 11, 272 pages, $19.95)

Licensing Art and Design, Revised Edition
by Caryn R. Leland (paperback, 6 × 9, 128 pages, $16.95)

Successful Syndication: A Guide for Writers and Cartoonists
by Michael Sedge (paperback, 6 × 9, 192 pages, $16.95)

Mastering 3D Animation, Second Edition with CD-ROM
by Peter Ratner (paperback, 8 × 9⅞, 352 pages, $40.00)

To request a free catalog or order books by credit card, call 1-800-491-2808. To see our complete catalog on the World Wide Web, or to order online for a 20 percent discount, you can find us at ***www.allworth.com.***